FINDING
MYSELF
ALONE

POSITIVE THOUGHTS, INSIGHTS,
AND DISCOVERIES OF LDS SINGLES

FINDING
MYSELF
ALONE

COMPILED AND EDITED BY
MICHAEL AGRELIUS AND
TAYLOR HALVERSON, PH.D.

ISBN 13: 978-1-951341-00-8

Published by Line of Sight Publishing.

Cover image © 2019
Cover design © 2019 by Shawnda Craig
Copyedited by Deborah Spencer

Dedicated to
All of the children, spouses (and former spouses),
parents, in-laws, and extended families of
everyone who contributed to this book,
or who has cause to read this book.

Contents

"I have heard thy prayer, I have seen thy tears: behold, I will heal thee." (2 Kings 20:5)

Introduction & Acknowledgments

I know you sometimes think that the rest of the Church can't relate to singles because they haven't gone through a divorce, lost a spouse, or struggled never finding the right someone at the right time. The truth is very seldom does a married couple depart this earth life at exactly the same moment. Thus more than half of the membership of the Church will eventually find themselves being single again."

These thoughts were spoken at a Single Adult Family Home Evening group. Singles are, unfortunately, one of the fastest growing segments of The Church of Jesus Christ of Latter-day Saints. In recent years even some of our dear prophets and members of the Quorum of the Twelve have found themselves temporarily single. With so many joining our ranks at this time in the history of the world, there must be things we are to learn.

Hopefully you will be inspired by learning some of the positive things that have come to others in similar circumstances. Perhaps you will receive some degree of encouragement that will help you to hold fast to what you know to be true, to continue the good fight, and to seek to know what your Father's will is concerning you and your present situation.

The opportunity is before us to "inherit thrones, kingdoms, principalities, and powers, dominions, all heights and depths . . . from everlasting to everlasting" (Revelation 1:6, 5:10. See also Moses 1; and D&C 132). What glorious promises and possibilities are before us!

Finding Myself Alone is a compilation of positive thoughts, insights, and discoveries made by single members of The Church of Jesus Christ of Latter-day Saints, who come with a variety of experiences but have all found themselves alone in this very family-oriented church. We express gratitude to a variety of organizations that helped us find those with stories to tell: *Fun For Less Tours, LDSsingles.com, LDSmingle.com,* and *LDSMatchup.com.* Thanks for encouragement and future promotions also goes to *LDS Matchup, Cruise Lady,* and the *Learn Our Religion Lecture Series.* We appreciate Rachel (Mike's daughter) who retyped many of these stories. It was a great blessing for us to read through the many submissions and to note with each one that even within the most difficult trials and tribulations there always seems to be a "hope for a better world . . . which hope cometh of faith . . . being led to glorify God" (Ether 12:4).

We express gratitude to all who have taken the time to write their thoughts and stories, and who have been willing to share these personal insights and discoveries. Readers should note that the individual tone and voice of each contributor have been preserved as much as possible so that their authentic experiences and expressions shine through.

We have divided this book into five sections for the convenience of the reader. Section one contains insights for anyone who has been or is currently single. Section two has stories for those yet to marry. Section three is for those who are divorced or thinking about it. Section four shares thoughts for those widowed. Section five contains concluding and encouraging thoughts.

In creating these five sections, we do not wish to categorize the pains, hurts, and challenges of being single. We also do not wish to imply that this book is only for singles. We think there are great things to learn from anyone who has experienced, overcome, or is striving to overcome, trials and tribulations—which seems to be everyone who has ever walked on this earth (yes, including prophets, and especially the Savior). "To him that overcometh will I grant to sit with me in my throne, even as I also overcame, and am set down with my Father in his throne" (Revelation 3:21).

We are honored to have had friends and strangers entrust with us their experiences and personal stories of being alone, and to have been willing to allow us to share them with you.

Here's hoping that some of these words will help you on your journey.

—Michael Agrelius and Taylor Halverson, Ph.D.

Cast Your Faith into the Wind

Cast your faith into the wind,
> *open up and smile again.*
It's not as bad as it appears,
> *there's still time, forget your fears.*

Skip your hopes across the sea,
> *fill your cup and let's be free.*
It's not as bad as it seems,
> *there's still time, dream your dreams.*

> *—m. agrelius*

Section One

Thoughts, Insights & Discoveries for Everyone

"There are only two ways to live your life.
One is as though nothing is a miracle.
The other is as though everything is a miracle."
(Albert Einstein)

Chapter One

The Three-Day Rule

BY TARA MARIA AMAVI

Editors' Note: Great advice on how to deal with challenges.

Here is the single most powerful truth I have learned, and it is not limited to the scope of singles or single life. I learned an important lesson about how to deal with the most extreme "opportunities to grow," the stuff others call tragedy, crisis, divorce, abandonment, trauma, ad infinitum. It's called the *Three-Day Rule*. I simply wait three days and see what has changed.

Now, whenever anything threatens my peace, my joy, my equanimity, I invoke the *Three-Day Rule* by asking myself two very simple questions:

1. What was the darkest hour in history? The day our Savior was crucified.
2. What was the brightest moment in history? Our Savior's resurrection day.

Why does asking these two questions comfort and redirect me? They comfort and redirect me because the answers to these questions demonstrate a powerful and recurring theme when it comes to coping with the illusion of tragedy.

Tie a knot, hang on, and just breathe. In three days, everything will have changed.

Editors' Take: Amen.

"When you face adversity, you can be led to ask many questions. Some serve a useful purpose; others do not. To ask, 'Why does this have to happen to me? Why do I have to suffer this now? What have I done to cause this?' will lead you into blind alleys. It really does no good to ask questions that reflect opposition to the will of God. Rather ask, 'What am I to do? What am I to learn from this experience? What am I to change? Whom am I to help?'" (Richard G. Scott)

Chapter Two

On Getting Lost

BY SUE GALLACHER

Editors' Note: Great attitude on how to approach life in general—especially single life.

I get lost all the time. Even with an electronic map that starts at my front door and tells me when to turn right and when to turn left and how many miles it is from the freeway to the frontage road, I can take a wrong turn somewhere and end up nowhere. This used to really stress me out, mostly because I hated being late for everything. Then I hit on the brilliant plan of giving myself an extra fifteen minutes every time I went someplace in order to have time "to get lost." It was like I was giving myself permission to get lost! It was great.

All of a sudden, it was in the transcript, it was on the program. Getting lost was part of the plan. So I didn't stress out about it anymore. I started actually—OK, this is going to sound weird—looking forward to it. It was the adventure of discovering the unknown and unexpected and going places I had never planned to go. Why, I was disappointed if I didn't get lost!

Now you know what I'm talking about here is getting lost in my car when I'm driving someplace, but you've probably also figured out by now that I've taken a few wrong turns in the romance department in my travels through life. But, since I've finally learned that getting lost just means *finding yourself in a different place than you thought you'd be in*, I've decided to relax and give myself a little extra time to enjoy the sights on this adventure, too.

Getting lost is part of the plan—at least part of *my* plan. It has brought me here, to a place I've never been before. And, maybe, this is exactly where I am supposed to be right now.

Editors' Take: Enjoy the journey and where you find yourself at this moment. It could (and will) all change.

"Patience is not indifference. Actually it is caring very much, but being willing, nevertheless, to submit both to the Lord and to what the scriptures call the 'process of time.' Patience is tied very closely to faith in our Heavenly Father. Actually, when we are unduly impatient, we are suggesting that we know what is best—better than does God. Or at least, we are asserting that our timetable is better than his." (Neal A. Maxwell)

Chapter Three

Discovering My New Nauvoos

by Taylor Halverson

Editors' Note: "The early Saints never thought that they would leave their Zion or Nauvoo and were deeply traumatized by the aloneness they experienced in having their Zion broken before their eyes. . . ." So it is with relationships.

Soon after finding myself newly alone, I visited Nauvoo, that city of Zion to which tens of thousands of Saints flocked in order to find community, peace, life, joy, and purpose. They did not want to be alone. And so they gathered from all quarters of the world to the City Beautiful, which is the meaning of the word *Nauvoo* in Hebrew.

The early Saints put everything they had into their beautiful new city. They had no expectation that their Nauvoo would fail, that their experiment with Zion would fail. And yet it did. It wasn't all their doing. But the Saints were gone and so was their dream. So, they turned to God in faith and trust, and they waited upon the Lord.

I did not go to Nauvoo to find myself again. I did not go to Nauvoo to overcome my loneliness. I went because it was an opportunity to learn more about Church history, to see the buildings of the early Latter-day Saint faith, to hear the sights and sounds, to feel the humidity rippling off the muddy Mississippi, to see the dappled light on the vibrant trees that lined the square-gridded streets. I was seeking to experience and understand the faith of the early Saints as best I could.

I was surprised that in seeking a collective past of faith I found myself again.

During that visit to Nauvoo I was reminded by the Spirit repeatedly that God knows each of us individually. I was reassured in unmistakable ways that God will reach out to each one of His beloved children in love and that they would *all* feel and recognize His love at some point in their lives. That was so immeasurably comforting to me. For some reason, in my own suffering, in my own loneliness, in my own broken state, I felt not only the searing reality of my own pain, but as I contemplated the untold numbers of people the world over who had suffered in agony, not perhaps my agony, but their own personal, exquisite suffering, my heart also broke for them. I had finally experienced true, long-lasting suffering and pain, the type that did not seem to provide an expiration date, the type of suffering made worse by not knowing when it would ever end. Knowing of my own suffering and now feeling how others have suffered, do currently suffer, and will suffer, I ached in my soul not just for personal comfort, but for comfort to know that others could be comforted too.

The clear and unmistakable response from God was that yes indeed, all of His children will individually feel of His love and recognize that love as divine.

On the streets of Nauvoo, I felt a surge of peace and joy, to be connected to God, to be connected to the faithful past. So strange that those feelings of healing were met by the silence of those streets. Where were the faithful? Where were their songs? Their meetings? Their work? Their families?

The faithful of Nauvoo have long since left their beautiful city. They left it alone.

But how could that be? I wondered. This was the promised city of Zion! This was the city that the faithful from around the world streamed to on the wings of God's protection with the songs of Zion's joy on their lips. Why were the faithful of Zion no longer in Nauvoo?

At that moment of questioning, God inspired my mind with a profound truth that healed my thinking about my own loneliness. "I have taken them to other Nauvoos, to new Zions."

I had been so caught up in what I thought was my life plan, having arrived at "my Nauvoo," that when I had to leave "my Nauvoo" behind I couldn't conceive that God had a much larger plan of growth, learning, experience, opportunity, and ultimately joy for me to find new Nauvoos, new Zions that I had never expected.

Just as the early Saints never thought that they would leave their Zion or Nauvoo and were deeply traumatized by the aloneness they experienced in having their Zion broken before their eyes, so too it was with me. My life did not foresee that my Nauvoo might be broken. However, in trusting in God, I would find new Nauvoos, new Zions, through which I could continue to grow in the light and love of God.

God led the early Saints from one Zion (Nauvoo) to a new Zion in the great American West. There they have flourished beyond all imagination. Their tears have been dried and their safety has been secured. The Saints of God are no longer alone. He is with them in their Zion. I realized God will be with me as I make my way to new Nauvoos and new Zions. The journey is part of the process which I signed up for in the premortal life. Without the suffering and the journey, I can never know the full joy of salvation through Jesus or ever become like my Father in Heaven.

Editors' Take: We work on and try to build our relationships as if they are forever, but often times things change. God is still directing us; we can still hear His word. New lands of promise can be realized.

"In everyone's life, at some time, our inner fire goes out. It is then burst into flame by an encounter with another human being. We should all be thankful for those people who rekindle the inner spirit." (Albert Schweitzer)

Chapter Four

Your Awakening

BY GOSH

Editors' Note: This speaks to the hope and encouragement that is needed to face most challenges, be they divorce, loss, yearning, or just facing everyday life.

There comes a time in your life when you finally get it. When in the midst of all your fears and insanity you stop dead in your tracks and somewhere the voice inside your head cries out *"Enough!"* Enough fighting and crying or struggling to hold on.

And, like a child quieting down after a blind tantrum, your sobs begin to subside, you shudder once or twice, you blink back your tears, and through a mantle of wet lashes, you begin to look at the world through new eyes.

This is your awakening.

You realize that it's time to stop hoping and waiting for something to change or for happiness, safety, and security to come galloping over the next horizon.

You come to terms with the fact that he is not Prince Charming and you are not Cinderella, that in the real world there aren't always fairytale endings (or beginnings, for that matter) and that any guarantee of "happily ever after" must begin with you. And, in the process, a sense of serenity is born of acceptance.

You awaken to the fact that you are not perfect and that not everyone will always love, appreciate, or approve of who or what you are. And that's OK. They are entitled to their own views and opinions.

You learn the importance of loving and championing yourself and gain a sense of newly-found confidence born of self-approval. You stop complaining and blaming other people for the things they did to you (or didn't do for you), and you learn that the only thing you can really count on is the unexpected.

You learn that people don't always say what they mean or mean what they say and that not everyone will always be there for you and that it's not always about you.

So you learn to stand on your own and to take care of yourself and along the way a sense of safety and security is born of self-reliance. You stop judging and pointing fingers and you begin to accept people as they are and to overlook their shortcomings and human frailties and in the process a sense of peace and contentment is born of forgiveness. You realize that much of the way you view yourself, and the world around you, is the result of all the messages and opinions that have been ingrained into your psyche.

And you begin to sift through all the junk you've been fed about how you should behave, how you should look, and how much you should weigh. What you should wear and where you should shop and what you should drive how and where you should live and what you should do for a living, who you should marry and what you should expect of a marriage, or what you owe your parents.

You learn to open up to new worlds and different points of view. And you begin reassessing and redefining who you are and what you really stand for. You learn the difference between wanting and needing and you begin to discard the false ideas and values you've outgrown, or should never have accepted to begin with. In the process you learn to go with your instincts.

You learn that it is truly in giving that we receive. And that there is power and glory in creating and contributing, and you stop maneuvering through life merely as a "consumer" looking for your next fix. You learn that principles such as honesty and integrity are not the outdated ideals of a bygone era but the mortar that holds together the foundation upon which you must build a life.

You learn that you don't know everything, that it's not your job to save the world, and that you can't teach a pig to sing. You learn to distinguish between guilt and responsibility and the importance of setting boundaries and learning to say "no."

Then you learn about love.

You learn about romantic love and familial love, how to love, how much to give in love, when to stop giving, and when to walk away. You learn not to project your needs or your feelings onto a relationship. You learn that you will not be more beautiful, more intelligent, more lovable, or more important because of the man on your arm or the child that bears your name.

You learn to look at relationships as they really are and not as you would have them be. You stop trying to control people, situations, and outcomes. You learn that just as people grow and change, so it is with love, and you learn that you don't have the right to demand love on your terms, just to make you happy.

And, you learn that alone does not mean lonely.

You look in the mirror and come to terms with the fact that you will never be a size five or a perfect ten and you stop trying to compete with the image inside your head and agonizing over how you "stack up." You also stop working so hard at putting your feelings aside, smoothing things over, or ignoring your needs.

You learn that feelings of entitlement are perfectly okay and that it's your right to want things and to ask for the things that you want and that sometimes it is necessary to make demands. You come to the realization that you deserve to be treated with love, kindness, sensitivity, and respect, and that you won't settle for less. And you allow only the hands of a lover who cherishes you to glorify you with his touch and in the process you internalize the meaning of self-respect.

And you learn that your body really is your temple. And you begin to care for it and treat it with respect. You begin eating a balanced diet, drinking more water, and taking more time to exercise. You learn that fatigue diminishes the spirit and can create doubt and fear. So you take more time to rest. And, just as food fuels the body, laughter fuels our soul. So you take more time to laugh and to play. You learn that, for the most part, in life you get what you believe you deserve and that much of life truly is a self-fulfilling prophecy. You learn that anything worth achieving is worth working for and that wishing for something to happen is different from working toward making it happen.

More importantly, you learn that in order to achieve success you need direction, discipline, and perseverance. You also learn that no one can do it all alone and that it's okay to risk asking for help. You learn that the only thing you must truly fear is the great robber baron of all: Time. *Fear* it.

You learn to step right into and through your fears because you know that whatever happens you can handle it and to give in to fear is to give away the right to live life on your terms. And you learn to fight for your life and not to squander it living under a cloud of impending doom. You learn that life isn't always fair, that you don't always get what you think you deserve, and that sometimes bad things happen to unsuspecting, good people. On these occasions you learn not to personalize things. You learn that God isn't punishing you or failing to answer your prayers. It's just life happening.

And you learn to deal with evil in its most primal state: The ego. You learn that negative feelings such as anger, envy, and resentment must be understood and redirected or they will suffocate the life out of you and poison the universe that surrounds you.

You learn to admit when you are wrong and to build bridges instead of walls. You learn to be thankful and to take comfort in many of the simple things we take for granted, things that millions of people upon the earth can only dream about: a full refrigerator; clean running water; a soft, warm bed; a long, hot shower.

Slowly you begin to take responsibility for yourself by yourself and you make yourself a promise to never betray yourself and never, ever to settle for less than your heart's desire.

You hang a wind chime outside your window so you can listen to the wind. And you make it a point to keep smiling, to keep trusting, and to stay open to every wonderful possibility.

Finally, with courage in your heart and with God by your side, you take a stand, you take a deep breath, and you begin to design the life you want to live as best as you can.

Editors' Take: This chapter was written for a friend who was having a tough time. God gives us gifts—friends to support us, a new day to use however we choose, an intellect to look for the positive in what we do and think about. It is up us to accept the gifts we are given to bring joy into the lives of others and ourselves.

"If you're going through hell, keep going." (Winston Churchill)

Chapter Five

The Prize

BY JAMIE BROMLEY

Editors' Note: Enjoy the journey no matter how difficult it can become.

I've always said, I'm not a swimmer. I took lessons as a child, like most of us do, but somewhere between the lessons and spending the summers at the beach, body surfing in the waves, I lost the ability to swim. So I'll say it again, I'm not a swimmer and I really know it now.

The test came recently when I did my first sprint triathlon. For five years I had the goal to compete in a triathlon. I decided that I would either do it the following summer or not at all. But you see the challenge was that I didn't swim, and I wasn't a runner either. So why would I want to do something so outrageous? My thought process was that it would offer a great method of cross-training in several disciplines. I thought it would be fun.

I began with the running and advanced from simply walking to being able to run a few 5Ks. I'm not a serious competitor but I was comfortable with the running. To get ready I had lots of what I call cheerleaders. I had a personal trainer, James, help me several times a week. His silent nature always let me know that he believed I could do anything that I set my mind to do. He always increased the weights or pushed me a little further than our previous session. I made progress by leaps and bounds. My first 5K, I took Emily, my fourteen-year-old niece. What a great cheerleader she is to me. She would run backward so that she was in front of me, encouraging me along the way by clapping her hands and telling me, "You can do it." She amazed me. I still see her clapping her hands and telling me, "You can do it."

To get ready I began taking swimming lessons, but I still wasn't getting the hang of it. As the date neared when I was going to be tested to swim, I became fearful. (Needless to say, I didn't win the triathlon, but I did it and had fun. What is important is the experience that I had.)

The day of the race, I stood out facing the swim course with a decision to make. What was my motivation? Did I want to do the triathlon only if I knew that I would do well, or did I want to do it because I had set a goal and it was within hours of being accomplished? I decided that I wanted to do it simply because it was a goal and I would have failed had I not tried. I wished my friends luck and we started our race. It turns out that I was in the water twice as long as the average swimmers. Fortunate for me there were kayakers all along the course for struggling swimmers.

Again, there I found cheerleaders, strangers reassuring me that it was worth the challenge, that I could do it and that the recorded time isn't important, it's about the experience. I was far behind the other contenders when I finally got out of the water. I was tired. My heart was beating too fast and I couldn't get it to lower. I found that I couldn't regulate my breathing. I was a little scared. But I reminded myself that I was accomplishing a goal.

I ran to hop on my bike and truly realized that I had no one to compete against because I couldn't see anyone in front of me. There were still swimmers behind me but I found myself alone. As I began the race, luck would have it that I had a wheel problem. The brake was dragging and I couldn't get it resolved. But still I rode on. As I went on the fifteen-mile bike race, I found myself forgetting that I was in a competition; at moments it was just another bike ride watching the scenery go by. The bike course was an in-and-out path, which did enable me to see several of my friends pass and we cheered each other on and encouraged each other to keep going as we were nearing the finish line. But still, I was alone and with no cheerleaders by my side, I had to find a way to accomplish my goal. I began seeing and hearing the recording in my mind of Emily clapping her hands and telling me, "You can do it." I knew of James' silent encouragement of pushing me just a little harder than the time before. I began cheering myself on. On a difficult hill, when I felt my strength weaken further, I yelled at the top of my lungs in unison with Emily in my mind, "Go, go, go!" It worked. I went faster up that hill than I had pedaled on the flat portions. As my solitary bike race progressed, I found that I was becoming my greatest cheerleader. Yet I wasn't really alone. I knew that there would be plenty family and friends at the finish line when I crossed. They were cheering me on, and I knew it. I just couldn't hear it.

I finished my bike ride and darted off for my four-mile run. One more step closer to the goal. Again, I was alone. I was tired and still felt beat by the swim; my breathing was still off and my heart still racing. I thought once, *Skip through these trees and catch up with the other runners ahead of you*. But I thought, *Why cheat yourself of an honest race?* Another thought I had was *What's the point?* And I remembered it was a goal and honestly thought, *You're having fun! Why quit now?* I struggled, but I didn't quit.

The fun really came at the finish line. Many friends were there and many strangers, not to necessarily cheer me on to the finish line, but to cheer on their children. Yes, I was so late I had merged in with the children's race. How exciting it was for me to come through with all of those cheers after a long race, a difficult race, one that needed me to cheer myself on to the finish line.

You know, life is just like my sprint triathlon. There are times where we need to be our own cheerleader, but we also have many cheerleaders and supporters helping us along our way in life. I've been able to add to the recordings in my mind the cheerleaders at the finish line; I know what their encouragement sounds like now.

There are times in our lives where we are forced to be our own cheerleaders. But more importantly, we need to remember that in our life race, our greatest cheerleader is the Lord. We must believe in the plan of happiness our Heavenly Father has set up for us. We have scores of family and friends at the "finish line" of our life, cheering us on. But we need to be believing and have faith. We need to keep in perspective what our motivation is. I believe that our greatest accomplishments can come when we push ourselves and we overcome whatever challenge we have in life. It's then, at that moment, that we truly realize how strong we are, that we can accomplish anything, as these two scriptures attest:

> *But this one thing I do, forgetting those things which are behind, and reaching forth unto those things which are before, I press toward the mark for the prize. (Phil. 3:13–14)*

> *For it is not requisite that a man should run faster than he has strength. And again, it is expedient that he should be diligent, that thereby he might win the prize. (Mosiah 4:27)*

Editors' Take: "There are times in our lives where we are forced to be our own cheerleaders. But more importantly, we need to remember that in our life race, our greatest cheerleader is the Lord."

"Choices are not always easy to see clearly. You make choices every day and almost every hour that keep you walking in the light or moving away toward darkness. Some of the most important choices are about what you set your heart upon."
(Henry B. Eyring)

Chapter Six

Jesus Became Like Us So We Could Become Like Him

BY TAYLOR HALVERSON

Editors' Note: Jesus was alone when He suffered, and sometimes we must suffer as well. However, lonely as we may be, we need not suffer alone.

I spent several years at the Yale University Divinity School. In that academic environment, I gained a lot of experience in biblical languages, texts, customs, and interpretations, as well as in theology, religious history, and religious traditions. But I most value what I learned through my relationships and conversations with others.

For a bit of context, the Yale University Divinity School is an ecumenical, multidenominational academic institution that trains scripture scholars and future ministers. There are

many divinity schools in North America, though most of
them are decidedly sectarian. That is, they admit students
from only a single faith tradition who are then taught by
professors who share that faith tradition, with the intent
that those students will serve in a variety of roles within that
faith tradition. Yale Divinity School is non-sectarian. It pro-
actively admits students from a variety of faith traditions,
which creates a vibrant ecumenical setting where conversations of learning and faith from a variety of perspectives
permeates the experience.

Most people who go to divinity school have the inten-
tion of being ordained and then entering the religious pro-
fession. So my friends at divinity school were amused when
they had this initial conversation with me.

Yale friend: So, are you hoping to become an
ordained minister?

Taylor: Actually, I'm already an ordained elder in
The Church of Jesus Christ of Latter-day Saints.

Yale friend (with some confusion): OK, so will you get
a paid ministry once you complete your Yale degree?

Taylor: Actually, no, on two points. First, there are
no paid clergy in The Church of Jesus Christ of
Latter-day Saints. Second, the church is run by a
lay clergy, so all positions are staffed by appointed
volunteerism.

My Yale friends were typically surprised that I would
attend a divinity school when I was already ordained in a

faith tradition that had no paid ministers. This would be analogous to a certified dentist, who provides free dental care to anyone who asks, paying to spend several years completing a degree at a dental school.

These types of conversations created opportunities for each of us to learn more about our faith, our religious traditions, and our aspirations for making a positive difference in the world. The Yale Divinity School was a residential academic program, so as students, we spent a lot of time together. We'd have classes together in the morning, then chapel service, more classes, and then lunch, with additional classes in the afternoon.

Lunchtime at Yale Divinity School was always special. Given the ecumenical nature of the divinity school, we all had a lot to discuss over the lunch table as we reviewed what we learned in our courses and asked each other how our individual faith traditions brought perspective to what we were learning.

It was in this ecumenical setting at Yale that I gained a major insight while in conversation with a fellow student. My friend shared his love for and perspective on Jesus Christ. I learned the following things from my friend:

For all that Jesus taught us, one of the most important things is that Jesus taught us how to suffer.

For all the difficulty, trial, and trauma of our lives, no one has suffered more than Jesus. No one has been more fully betrayed, more fully misunderstood, more fully alone.

Jesus wasn't simply alone in his suffering. He was totally alone while he suffered the exquisite infinity of all pain—all for us.

As I reflected on these insights from my friend, I realized Jesus suffered so that we may not have to suffer in the same way. When we do suffer, he is our exemplar for patient, faithful, pleading, enduring suffering. When we experience such suffering in our lives, it is then that one of the most oft-used scriptural phrases that seems so innocuously pedestrian becomes the most soothing balm of Gilead: "And it came to pass."

Notice that this phrase is not "And it came to stay." The pain and troubles all will pass. They will never permanently stay. Our suffering is finite. Our difficulties come to pass in order that we might learn and know. Thus, without suffering, there is no preparation for learning. And without the Atonement to heal all, there is no true learning.

In our suffering, we come to experience the truth and reality that Jesus became like us so that we could become like him. God—who knew all, had all, created all—was willing to take on the destructive flesh of a mortal body to suffer with us, live with us, love us, and thereby show us a better way.

Editors' Note & Take: The infinite Atonement provides us with finite suffering that we can overcome to allow us to become like our Savior. This chapter was originally published by Taylor Halverson in the *Deseret News*. Republished with permission.

*"Our greatest glory is not in never falling,
but in rising every time we fall." (Confucius)*

Chapter Seven

Measuring Up

BY SUE GALLACHER

Editors' Note: Comparisons do not end well on so many levels.

I dated a guy once who just loved to talk about his ex-girlfriends. Since I didn't have that many ex-boyfriends at the time to talk about, and also since I was pretty fascinated by anything that fascinated him, I mostly just listened. He never said anything negative about them and he was never indiscreet; in fact, he was very respectful and seemed to have loved all of them pretty equally. And he never told me their names; they all had nicknames. There was "Golf Girl" and "36" and "Miss L.A." and even one called "The Perfect Body."

She was the one he liked to talk about the most, and I would pay rapt attention to his wistful descriptions of her lovely shape, form, and dimensions. Apparently, she had walked away from their relationship leaving nothing but a complete mystery behind. My boyfriend, who we'll call

Bob, had no idea what happened or why she left. All he knew was that she was now engaged to another man and was going to be getting married soon.

I ended up really falling for this man and, even though he still appeared to be a little hung up on Miss Perfect Body, it seemed to me that we had a pretty good shot at a really great future together. After all, we both loved to read the scriptures and sing and speak Spanish and eat See's raspberry creams. We both had three kids who were about the same ages and into the same kinds of things, and we even both had sons serving missions in the same mission in Mexico City. And what's more, neither one of us had the perfect body.

But just when it looked as if the time were right to spring the three magic words on him about how I felt, he wanted to have "a talk." Now, that is usually not a good thing, but I had no idea how bad this talk was going to be. For me.

"Honey," he said, "I don't know how to say this, so I'm just going to come right out and tell you everything. My ex-girlfriend came back to me last night. She showed up on my doorstep and said she couldn't go through with her wedding because she realized she was still in love with me. I couldn't believe it—I hadn't seen her in almost a year. I'm so confused because I have real feelings for you and I don't want to hurt you. But I have history with this woman and I feel like I have to give my relationship with her a second chance."

What could I say? I only had one question.

"Is it The Perfect Body?" I whispered.

"Yes," he said worshipfully, "and it's as perfect as ever."

How could I argue with *that*? "Go to her. I wish you all the best," I said. "I can *not* compete with that."

I think I cried a little over losing him. I can't really remember, because mostly what I do remember was getting pretty mad at him after I gave it some thought. How shallow can you get—he dumped me for someone else because she had a better body? Oh, yeah? Well, I could get one of those, too, and then I would show him what he gave up, and, boy, would he be sorry. I joined the gym and hired a walking tree trunk of a personal trainer named Octavius.

I told Octavius the whole story—all the details about the wonderful relationship, the See's candies, The Perfect Body, and the "talk." He was mad about it, too.

"He shouldn't do you that way," he said, "especially since you have the raw materials to have a perfect body of your own." I liked the way Octavius talked. "I will sculpt you," he promised, and I willingly placed myself in his hands.

Months later, after three to four sessions a week with The Octopus, as they called him, and gallons of daily protein shakes, I had lost thirteen pounds of "body fat." But the scale only showed a six-pound loss. Octavius took my measurements again and pinched my arm with his little plastic caliper and explained the whole muscle-weighs-more-than-fat theory one more time. I had to admit my pants were looser and my shirt sleeves were tighter due to the little bulgy muscles in my arms, but when I looked in the mirror, I still did *not* see the perfect body.

"You look fantastic," Octavius said when I mentioned my lack of perfection. "For your age," he added. Did he have to add that? For who knew how old The Perfect Body was? She could be my age too and yet still be perfect. Although, admittedly, she probably was a lot younger. Sigh.

I went home that day feeling pretty defeated. I wouldn't be able to show up and surprise Bob the way I had planned. I wouldn't be able to show off a body chiseled to perfection like his old girlfriend's. I would never have a perfect body.

The phone rang, and I answered it without looking at the caller's name. It was Bob!

"Hi, baby! I've missed you. Have you missed me?" he chirped cheerfully, as light and breezy as if he had just been off at a golf tournament in Barbados for a weekend or something.

"Of course," I answered. "How are you?"

"Not so good," he responded, the cheer in his voice silenced.

"Umm, what's wrong?" I asked, hoping that his heart had been broken—no, smashed—into a million painful, jagged pieces. "Is everything OK with your girlfriend, the one with the perfect body?" I held my breath.

"Oh, her," he replied, almost offhandedly. "That didn't work out."

"*What*?!" I exhaled explosively, "What do you mean? She had the *perfect body*!"

"Yes, but one day, when we were sitting in church together—it was when they read the letter from the prophet admonishing us to read The Book of Mormon again before the end of the year—I turned to her and asked her if she would read it together with me, and she said, 'No, why should I? I've already read it.' And I thought to myself, '*Sue* would do it, Sue would want to, she loves The Book of Mormon.' And so I broke things off with her."

"Because of The Book of Mormon???"

"No, silly, because of *you*. She just couldn't measure up to you. She never would be able to."

Needless to say, I learned a big lesson from this little romantic episode in my life. I learned that having a perfect body isn't everything. But mostly what I learned was that I had been evaluating myself by the wrong measuring stick. I had realized that by "measuring themselves by themselves, and comparing themselves among themselves, [I was] not wise" (2 Corinthians 10:12). I had judged myself in a way that Bob had not. I had made assumptions about my inadequacies that I should not have made. I made a vow to myself then and there not to compare myself to anybody again, and especially not to compare myself to people whose nicknames had the word "perfect" in them.

Oh, and by the way, I did not go back to Bob. Although we remain friends, I went on to date my own version of The Perfect Body, who taught me another lesson I like to call "Getting What You Ask For," but that's a whole different episode in my *Book of Love Lessons Learned the Hard Way*.

Editors' Take: There is no competition for the love and acceptance of the Lord.

"Look not at what you have lost, but at what you have left."
(Robert H. Schuller)

Chapter Eight

Pony Ride

BY BONNIE JOHNSON

Editors' Note: Ponies are like people: they're all different, and they're all worth getting to know.

I had a pony for a year when I was a kid. The dang thing was just plain mean and devised any plan it could think of to put me in the dirt and hurt me. It bucked me off, scraped me off on trees, ran off with me, kicked me, bit me, etc. I loved that dang 'lil pony. When my folks sold her, I cried. When the guy came to get her, he let me ride her one last time. And she bucked me off one last time. It was years later before I was able to have anything to do with horses again (not because I didn't want to). When I started riding again, I wasn't very good at it, but I loved it so I kept trying. I can't tell you how often I was on the ground thinking, *What just happened?!* My hubby was helpful and constantly explained to me all the things I was doing wrong and I tried so hard to do it right. He used to tell me, "If you're not coming off once in a while it's 'cause you're not riding hard enough." I got up early in the mornings and rode. I rode late at night under the lights. I wanted to be good. I wanted to do better. I hated kissing the dirt even worse than the slings and stitches that sometimes resulted from it.

And what did I learn?

Not all horses are the same. Some want to kill you, but most just want to be loved. Some are mean; others, real sweethearts. Some will work their butts off to please you; others won't move a muscle unless you make them. If you ride enough of them, you will see all kinds of personalities and dispositions. All in all though, *most* horses are an absolute pleasure to be around. I can't help but think how much I would have missed if I had judged all horses by the first pony I rode.

Therefore, I believe it's important to remember this: Not all people are the same and you can't judge one by your experiences with another. You should do whatever it takes to stay close to the Lord, because *you know you can trust Him*. Let Him lead you and guide you in your relationships. Don't be afraid to fall off now and then (it just means you *are* trying hard enough). Don't be afraid to love, and to trust, and to put it all out there. And if you do fall again, He will pick you up, stitch you up, provide the slings and bandages, and help you get back on and do it again. Eventually you will have what you are looking for, and it will be the *ride of your life!*

Editors' Take: Trust the Lord and trust that there are opportunities in all experiences.

"Everything will be okay in the end.
If it's not okay, it's not the end." (Unknown)

Section Two

Thoughts, Insights
& Discoveries for
Those Yet to Marry

"Never allow someone to be your priority while allowing yourself to be their option." (Mark Twain)

Chapter Nine

Finding Myself

BY JAMIE BOWLEY

Editors' Note: This story speaks of being alone, how to best deal with it, and how to best prepare for whatever comes our way.

F inding myself alone." That is a powerful statement. When I initially think of that individual statement, one word echoes in my mind: *alone*. I can hear it as if yelled in a tunnel, echoing until it fades to a whisper. That's how I've felt about being alone; echoes of experiences until they become a faded memory.

Alone usually implies unaccompanied, by yourself, or being unaided. It's all self-centered, or singular. I found being alone so difficult.

I've never been married but I realized I needed to adjust to being alone. But how? The easy answer is to be married, but I know through friends and family that one can be very alone in a marriage. So being married isn't the real answer to counter the echoes of alone. My reality is that I may never marry.

Finding myself alone has become a quest of finding myself. A few years ago in my late twenties, after yet another heartache, I had a good look at where I was. As I evaluated, I discovered that I often found myself waiting. Waiting for Mr. Right. Waiting to be rescued. Waiting for my turn. Just waiting. Those who know me, know that I don't like waiting. So what was I waiting for? I discovered that I was waiting to live. I was very active in life, but I'll say it again so that maybe you'll hear yourself: I was waiting to live. I had placed, through teachings of the Church and my own belief, too much weight on the idea that life started when I arrived, as if on a grand chariot, at who I thought I was supposed to be: a wife and mother. I was waiting to be a wife and mother. Somewhere I equated Mr. Right with my lifeline. As I made that realization, other realizations started falling into place. One of my next questions was, Did I want Mr. Right to be sitting at home "waiting" for me? No. When I allowed myself to be honest, I wanted Mr. Right to be living life, to have experiences, to have heartaches, to find himself so that he would be prepared for me. If that's what I wanted of him, I quickly discovered that I needed to do that for me. I had to find myself.

By my late twenties, I had been Relief Society president three times in different singles wards. You would think that I would have already found myself. But it was more than just having a testimony of the gospel and being able to serve. I soon enrolled myself back into school to receive my undergraduate degree. Soon after that, I discovered that I really wanted a graduate degree, which I painstakingly earned. In finding myself, I learned that truly how I treat family would be how I treat Mr. Right, so I started taking care with those special relationships. I discovered that I enjoy rock climbing, running, hiking, and maybe even triathlons. I learned that marriage is just a magnification of being single. My arrival on a grand chariot into motherhood hasn't occurred. However, I've learned that I can still fulfill my divine role as a woman by nurturing the young women that I teach and my nieces and nephews. Although external factors can play a large role, I've learned that happiness comes from within. I'm still learning and finding myself, but the alone isn't so bad.

In finding myself alone, I found myself. I found strength that I never knew that I had. I found that I am a confident woman. The process continues but I'm a much better woman now than I would have been if I were still waiting. The echo is being replaced with the resolve to find myself.

Editors' Take: Waiting for life to begin with an all-important someone isn't what God had in mind when He said we should seek to fill the measure of our creation. We need to be "actively engaged" in a good cause before—and whether—we actually become "actively engaged."

"Life is a sea upon which the proud are humbled, the shirker is exposed, and the leader is revealed. To sail it safely and reach your desired port, you need to keep your charts at hand and up-to-date. You need to learn by the experience of others, to stand firm for principles, to broaden your interests, to be understanding of the rights of others to sail the same sea, and to be reliable in the discharge of your duty." (Thomas S. Monson)

Chapter Ten

I'll Never Get Married

BY AL FOX CARRAWAY

Editors' Note: The saint sometimes called "The Tattooed Mormon" had a whole new set of challenges presented to her when she sought to keep all of God's commandments, including being married.

After I joined the Church, it was a long and incredibly lonely time before I would even be considered for a date, mostly because guys couldn't get past my appearance. And that was really hard, just barely moving to Utah against my will (but following God's), being in a new place, not knowing what I was supposed to do there, and feeling absolutely and completely alone. (No, not just because of the lack of boys, but in general and in every way you could probably think of). Guys my age were looking for temple worthy girls; however, I didn't exactly look temple worthy, so they didn't even speak to me. After my move across the country, it was the first time that it ever occurred to me that, appearance aside, my life before the Church could not only stop guys from wanting to date, but even keep them from wanting to be friends. I would notice the kind of girls that were getting asked out and I began to be afraid that because I didn't look "perfect," grow up in a strong Gospel-centered family, or know how to cook or make my own skirts, I was forever going to be overlooked.

A lesson I learned shortly after baptism—when I felt the weight of the world of problems come flooding into my life—was that if I continued to put God first, everything else would fall in to place.

I decided to stay focused on what really mattered to me, hoping that if I did, things would eventually work out how they ought to. If I stayed close to God, God will bless me. So I worried about *me* and the relationship I *did* have. With God. Things started to unfold in ways I never would have imagined. I started blogging and making YouTube videos and traveling all over the West giving devotionals, meeting hundreds of incredible people a day. I learned lessons I couldn't imagine living life without. I grew beyond what I thought I could in such a short time. I decided to receive my endowment, and a week after I did I became an ordinance worker in the Provo Temple.

Because I was speaking so often while working full time, I gave up my only date nights (Saturdays) to serve Him in His house. I would sit in the celestial room during my shift and see girls younger than me, married, nestled with their husbands—and couldn't help but be reminded that that wasn't me and probably won't be for a *long* while.

When I first got baptized and started to think about my husband I had those generic answers of, I wanted someone tall and could make me laugh. But really, that's not what was truly most important to me. There were plenty of tall, funny people, but what I wanted most of all was a spiritual attraction. There were things that I *needed* in a spouse, spiritually, that could *not* be overlooked. Someone whose most important relationship was not with me, but with God. I needed someone equal to if not stronger than me who could strengthen and help me on my weak days. I needed someone who could fully accept me, including my goals and independence. Someone who could completely accept where I came from and help me get to where I wanted to go in life with the Gospel.

The more time that passed the more I became disheartened. Was I expecting too much in a future companion? Was I being too picky? Did whom I need and want even exist? If not, what part was I willing to compromise? Would someone fully accept who I was and accept who I used to be? Accept the things I *can't* do and embrace the things I can?

I always thought I was expecting too much in someone and that I'd eventually have to settle with some qualities. Then many years later, this guy popped up out of nowhere! I honestly believe he came as a blessing to my efforts with the Lord. And we clicked just right. Because of him and his testimony and those qualities that were important to me, we find we work better as a team than we ever did on our own, and hard things in life are easier. I am grateful that I was patient enough to wait to meet him. I'd hate to think what life would be like if I wasn't. I hate to think of life without our experiences and laughs and lessons and our baby Gracie. I hate to think what I would have missed if I didn't trust God. Truth is, I'm not sure what kind of wife I'd be without the qualities and lessons and talents I developed while I was single and "waiting," because I am such a better person because of them.

I saw a question online once that asked: "What's the one thing that brings you the most joy?" and thought, "Easy, my husband." Then, "Wait—No—God. Wait—" And as I was thinking (much deeper than I think was intended), I realized how perfectly Heavenly Father has blessed me with Ben and how He uses him every day, a million times a day, to help and bless me and answer my prayers. I'm grateful for God and His ways and His all-knowing eye and guidance in my life. I'm nothing without God. And I'm incredibly grateful for my husband, his strengths, passion, humor, and patience in my life. But I'm mostly grateful for his love and joy that he also has on his own for God to truly make what we have incredible.

You will be blessed with a companion that will help you in the ways you need, even if sometimes you feel like that person doesn't exist or that you're asking for too much or that you're too picky. *Don't let passing time allow doubts and settling to take over.* Don't lose patience and miss out on what He has in store for you. Don't hold yourself back from learning and growing and experiencing other things. Just hold on and don›t lose confidence. Heavenly Father knows what's important to us and what we need.

Don't waste your thoughts comparing yourself and defining yourself by what you *aren't* and what others are.

Don't allow yourself to question what is "wrong with you." Heavenly Father did not shortchange or screw up on you. Don't stress. You just worry about you and worry about God. Because the thing about Heavenly Father is that if we are trying and are patient, we will never be short-changed from the best blessings He has to offer.

Yeah, sure our future can be uncertain at times, but how exciting that is! How exciting it is to know it's guided by God!

Happiness and unhappiness exist in the same exact place at the same time through different people. It's true, life is what you make it. Or it could be what *we allow* God to make of it for us. What will you choose? Choose happiness. And to choose happiness is to choose God. Choose to keep going. Choose to trust. Choose to have faith. To keep your hope. And choose to receive the unexpected, but profoundly greater, path with the best blessings. I promise, you'll be all right.

Editors' Note: Great advice to all as we contemplate marriage: "There were things that I *needed* in a spouse, spiritually, that could *not* be overlooked. Someone whose most important relationship was not with me, but with God. I needed someone equal to if not stronger than me who could strengthen and help me on my weak days." This chapter was originally published on Al Fox Carraway's blog, *In the Head of Al*, on February 6, 2015, at http://alfoxshead.blogspot.com/2015/02/ill-never-get-married.html. Republished with permission from the author.

*"No matter what your past has been,
you have a spotless future."* (Hugh B. Brown)

Chapter Eleven

On Marrying the "Tattooed Mormon"

BY BEN CARRAWAY

Editors' Note: Al's husband talks about what people said to him as he contemplated marriage, and how to look at people who have come into the gospel.

Oh, the words of advice we were given from people before we were married. They would say marriage is tough. Marriage is hard. Marriage is a battle. Marriage isn't easy. Are you sure you're ready? Your life is over. No more fun and games. Others would say that it was the best time of your life. A new adventure. A new beginning. True happiness. We've all heard them, right? I think being married to my wife has been the best thing that has ever happened to me.

A lot of people know my wife as the "Tattooed Mormon," though I must say I very much dislike that nickname for my wife. I have never been a big fan of the name "Tattooed Mormon" and she knows that. When we were engaged, people at her speaking events and even people I know would ask me, "How does it feel to marry a celebrity?" Or "How do you do it? How do you look past the tattoos she has, knowing that people will stare?" Some would even applaud me on marrying her, because of her past and how her past is so visual. I mean really? Serious? Hearing that used to bother me. Not once have I ever noticed or even cared that she has tattoos; I just don't see them when I look her. Sure, I know they are there, but it's not something I have ever cared about. When we were writing on my mission or when we were dating I would tell people about her, it was, "She is a blonde haired, blue-eyed girl, with a killer testimony and personality." Not ever was it, "Oh, I'm dating this girl with tattoos, with blonde hair and blue eyes." Because, to me, who cares if she has tattoos? It's not a big deal. That was part of her past, before she even became a member of the Church.

I don't think she should be defined or known by some as the "Tattooed Mormon." Sure she has tattoos and to some her past shows, but why should that define her? She is just like anyone in this Church. The greatest part of this Gospel is that people can change. She is a wonderful example of that! Boy, is she ever! She has shared with me how hard it was for her in Utah with people judging her for her tattoos, not giving her a chance. Pasts scare some people. But I love that about her.

I have a past that I'm not proud of, a past that took me years to overcome and years to cope with. I know very well now I have been forgiven and lots of blessings have come. I was always worried about who I would marry, because I thought who I used to be would be a roadblock for some girls. I always wanted to marry someone who knows me and accepts me and has a story of her own. I found her. I feel as though it's hard sometimes to let people change. Or doubting that they even can. This Church and Jesus Christ are about accepting anyone and everyone. No matter what they look like, no matter what they have done or where they have been. Christ is the master of change. He gives anyone who comes unto Him a new heart and a new mind. He is beautiful. He makes everyone beautiful, if they just trust in him and believe they can change.

Let pasts go. Allow people to show you that they can change, grow, and become better. My wife was called out for how she looked on her first day in Utah because she was tattooed and holding a church book. That guy told her how foolish she looked. That's messed up. When my wife and I meet people, a lot of the time I will notice their eyes just staring at her tattoos. To me she is not the "Tattooed Mormon" nor will she ever be in my eyes.

Marriage for us, I can firmly say, has not been hard one bit. Sure there have been life difficulties, but we get over them. I love her more and more every day. I love her more than the day I married her. I find her even more attractive than when we first met. I fall in love with her every day. Even to this day when I look in her deep blue eyes, I know why I married her. I married her not for her looks, sure that's a bonus, but I married her for *who* she is. I love who she is, where she came from, and what it took for her to get where she is today. I married way above myself. She keeps me corrected. She keeps me on the right course. Never marry because of looks and looks only. Marry someone who you are attracted to in every way, especially spiritually. Spiritual attraction is most important; that's what makes those hard things easier. Marry someone who has the same end goal in mind.

Sure my wife has tattoos and a lot of people stare, and some know her as the "Tattooed Mormon." But others know who my wife truly is. I love my wife and her courage to open her mouth to prove that people can change. I have. She has. We all can change. Don't let your appearance, your past, or whatever stop you from changing. Let people show you they can change; you never know what their potential is. Tattoos should never define someone. Pasts should never define someone. Christ died for our transgressions. If he forgets about them and doesn't notice us for what we have done, let us forget and forgive.

Editors' Note: "Allow people to show you that they can change, grow, and become better." This chapter was originally published on Ben Carraway's blog *The Way of Carraway* on May 9, 2014, at http://thewayofcarraway.blogspot.com/2014/05/being-married-to-tattooed-mormon.html. Republished with permission.

"To every thing there is a season . . . a time to weep, and a time to laugh; a time to mourn, and a time to dance; a time to cast away stones, and a time to gather stones together; a time to embrace, and a time to refrain from embracing; a time to get and a time to lose; a time to keep and a time to cast away." (Ecclesiastes 3:1–6)

Chapter Twelve

Enjoy Today

BY NANCY

Editors' Note: "Learn to enjoy your own company."

I've never been married. For many years of my single life I felt that I had to always be doing something, going somewhere, and not just be at home. I always had a roommate until about five years ago. One of those former roommates said there's nothing wrong with being at home and not always on the go. Take the time to be with yourself, to think and meditate about life. I think I was unconsciously being busy to not have the time to think about my life by myself.

My grandmother, a very wise person, told my mother, who became a widow at my age (forty-eight) to learn to enjoy your own company. My mother learned how to do that and I feel I have done the same. I am now in a place in my life where I love to be at home. I don't think of it anymore as being alone. I feel that this has been a growing experience and I even liken it to our lives here on this earth and our eternal salvation. Whatever level of salvation we attain after this life is really done by ourselves, alone (of course with the Lord). I still desire an eternal marriage and would appreciate the companionship in achieving those things that our Heavenly Father wants for us, but I know that my eternal salvation is ultimately up to me.

Editors' Take: Being comfortable with being single is akin to being comfortable being anywhere—including being in the presence of the Lord.

"Whether or not it is clear to you, no doubt the universe is unfolding as it should." (Max Ehrmann)

Section Three

Thoughts, Insights & Discoveries for Those Who Are Divorced or Are Thinking About Divorce

"Learn from yesterday. Live for today. Hope for tomorrow."
(Albert Einstein)

Chapter Thirteen

When Good People Get Divorced

BY DAN NONYMOUS

Editors' Note: "Being a good person, in spite of challenges, is what faith, grit, and integrity are all about."

What happens when good people get divorced? They keep being good people, that's what. They continue to do good things and generally do so as long as they live worthy to have the Spirit of the Lord. They continue to pray. In fact, they probably pray even more, study the scriptures, go to church, go to the temple, smile, and live the gospel. That is not to say that they don't struggle and have new sets of challenges. They do. Their children struggle, also have challenges, and all learn and grow.

Suffering, trials, and tribulations are part of our earth life experience. Challenges are not restricted to people who are married, get divorced, lose a spouse, or never get married.

These experiences happen to good people, bad people, and people who don't know who they are or what is happening to them. Challenges happen to the innocent and the guilty alike. Trials have not been a stranger to the likes of Moses, Abraham, Jacob, Joseph, Nephi, Abinadi, Alma, Peter, Paul, Joseph Smith, Spencer W. Kimball, Gordon B. Hinckley, Thomas S. Monson, the Savior, and countless others.

Being a good person, in spite of challenges, is what faith, grit, and integrity are all about.

Editors' Take: The Lord knows our hearts. He gives us agency for us to prove to *ourselves* that we are who *He* knows us to be.

"In order to be free, we must learn how to let go. Release the hurt. Release the fear. Refuse to entertain your old pain. The energy it takes to hang onto the past is holding you back from a new life. What is it you would let go of today?" (Mary Manin Morrissey)

Chapter Fourteen

Enough

BY Michael Agrelius

Editors' Note: Being "enough" may be tough to accomplish in this life, for others and even for ourselves. However, we won't be judged by "others," and the Perfect Judge has a bar not of this world.

When you read this title, what do you think? *Enough* can be taken so many different ways. Angrily, as in "I've had *enough*! I'm through!" Dejectedly, as in, "I guess that's enough. There's nothing left. I give up." And, perhaps the toughest of all, despairingly, "I'm never going to be *enough*."

Have you met people who seem to be placed in your life at certain times so that you could learn important lessons from them? I have. I did. Immediately after I was divorced I met a wonderful individual who opened my eyes and my heart to understanding things I couldn't seem to grasp on my own. She expressed the same feelings she had in her marriage with her former spouse as mine had done with me right before we divorced. The feeling was, "I'm never going to be enough for that person. I hope I can be enough for the next one." That and the other two *enoughs* as outlined above I am certain are all planted in our hearts by someone other than a kind and loving Father in Heaven.

My friend said she wanted to write a book on this subject. I hope she will because I loved our discussions on the subject and she has some brilliant and insightful thoughts about how to be enough. I won't use her ideas here but I will give you some of my thoughts on what is enough and how we achieve it with someone we love.

As I have now gone out with several different women since my divorce, I see that they, as well as many men (who don't seem to want to admit it quite as much), are all yearning to be "good enough," "beautiful/handsome enough," "spiritual enough" for that special someone. Most wish they could have been that "enough" for their former spouse. The truth of the matter is I'm not sure we can ever be enough to anyone in this life. Part of the problem is we often don't feel we are enough for ourselves. I think those feelings come in part from humility, in part from knowing our true potential, in part from comparisons with others, and in part from a misunderstanding of the gospel.

We are good enough, beautiful enough, and spiritual enough for our Father in Heaven (see Elder Jeffery Holland's October 2005 conference address "To Young Women"). Heavenly Father wants us just as we are. He wants us to become better, but He doesn't require it immediately. He knows that, in addition to repentance, improvement will take time, effort, probably tears, and most likely years. But He is patient, knows our divine potential, and has, through the sacrifice of His Son, provided a way (sorry, not "a way," The Way) to be clean, true, and complete.

We shouldn't get down on ourselves. The gospel is a message of light; it uplifts and inspires. The gospel is also a message of choice. We can choose to think that we are not enough for others. Or we can choose to believe that we are enough for the One who really counts and strive to be even more worthy to be called His sons and His daughters. "Be ye therefore perfect even as your Father in Heaven" was not achievable even for the Savior in this life. It wasn't until after His Resurrection that He included Himself in the statement.

I have been told by people much smarter than me that the Hebrew word "perfect" translates more closely to the English word "complete" than it does to the current Western definition of perfection. If we all understood the gospel, we would first know that our children, our spouses, our former spouses, those who have the possibility of being our spouses, our family, our friends, our enemies, and even we, ourselves, are all children of God. We would also know that we are all already enough for Him and should be enough for each other. We should be accepting, kind, and encouraging to everyone, including ourselves.

Editors' Take: We are enough for the One who counts. He invites us to come unto Him just as we are and He will make us whole, complete, perfect as He is.

"Happy is he that condemneth not himself in that thing which he alloweth." (Romans 14:22)

Chapter Fifteen

Thoughts on Being Alone

BY DIANE NONYMOUS

Editors' Note: Fear can trap us. Fear of being alone can trap us in our "aloneness."

I am forty-three years old and divorced at forty-one after almost twenty-two years of marriage, which began in the temple and at BYU. I have three children aged twelve, sixteen, and nineteen, and I was born into a family of eight children. My family are converts, and I was baptized at the age of eight. Honor, respect, education, and "saving face" were core values in my family. All but one (of my siblings) are very active members, including five returned missionaries, and I was the first and only one to be divorced (a serious "losing face").

"All alone."

My greatest fear of leaving my twenty-two–year marriage was of being alone with myself. Although my spouse had been unfaithful multiple times, I believe my willingness to overlook his indiscretions were rooted in this fear of being alone. Staying with him was better than the alternative of being left alone. Why was I so afraid to be alone? I was a lost soul. I did not know who I was and didn't like "me." Divorce meant I would be trapped with just me, alone. Although I have three children, I did not consider it their responsibility to be my lifetime companions and save me from my "aloneness."

Mind you, it took a long time to discover that, amongst many other good reasons to have stayed in our temple marriage, this unknown fear was the poorest reason. It was a reason that kept me chained, co-dependent, and in denial. It was a fear I wished I could have addressed while married, because it wasn't about my spouse at the time, it was about me. It was about my issues and fears of being alone. I would rather have had someone, as unhealthy as the relationship was, than to be left alone and by myself.

These things I share with you in the hopes that maybe it will awaken some hidden crevices in your pain and self-awareness that maybe have burdened you unknowingly (a.k.a. denial). I needed to muster the courage to risk and to venture into unforged territory, where I would either validate the awful truth that I truly was nothing or would discover my invaluable worth. Once I divorced I was on my own and I finally wanted to know the truth, harsh as it could be.

I didn't really know or like who I was. I didn't want to be left alone with a person like me. I saw my weaknesses and follies on a grand scale and had lost my vision that I was of any worth. Those shortcomings, over a period of my marriage, led to fear which I covered up by becoming controlling. I feared I really was of no worth. Although I was considered very accomplished, talented, and put together on the outside, underneath all of the exterior, I didn't believe it. I didn't even know who I was anymore, or maybe I never really did. Because of my extroverted personality, I liked being surrounded by people and never took the time to really find out who I was without them. I allowed others to define who I was. I had become a people pleaser.

But to my family, I became controlling, yet out of control. My relationship with my husband was crumbling. His choices destroyed my respect and trust in him. But at the same time he had become my self-worth. Now this false sense of identity was unmasked too. I had allowed that fake, "happy" outward appearance to be enough to sustain me.

Not any more though. Now, it was time to face my deepest fears. I would either fly as I had never known before or crash and burn permanently. A thread of hope kept me from giving up. With unanticipated support and encouragement, I finally left my marriage with incredible fear and intense trepidation.

Could I be happy with myself? It was time to find out the truth. It was finally time. Otherwise, I was sure to self-destruct. I could no longer keep up the false "happy face" persona.

I began to ask why I didn't like myself. I began an incredible journey in discovering the misconceptions I formed as a child in a home where my parents' constant criticism of me destroyed my inner sense of worth. I came to believe that my worth was weighed by my achievements and accomplishments. Despite many such "glories," still I felt inner emptiness and non-acceptance. I also felt unloved and believed myself to be unlovable. I have come to realize that my parents and I spoke different love languages. I needed affection and validation, while they showed their love for me through acts of service and providing for me. I did not understand that until this past year. For all those years, I truly believed I was unwanted, unloved, and unlovable. Who would want to be with me? Certainly not me! I denied those feelings for all those long forty-one years.

What a burden to carry to a marriage! Yet, the gospel truths of my divine nature were seeds just waiting to sprout. This became the time to discover, with my Heavenly Father's help, who I really was, if I was worth loving at all. The teachings of the gospel about who we are, which I had heard all my life, flickered a flame of hope that I might truly be worth something. Somehow, until this time I had believed that those teachings applied to everyone else, but not to me. Even though I knew the Spirit had told me such before, I still doubted. Now, I wished to doubt no longer, and I needed to know if Heavenly Father really loved me as His precious daughter, inwardly weak.

I went through a self-awareness learning process. I was so lost and didn't even know what I really liked to eat. I identified with Julia Roberts in the movie *Runaway Bride*, who didn't even know what kind of eggs she liked. Yes, I tried that too!

I began to spend more and more time alone walking, reading, praying, pondering, discovering. In fact, I have come to love and treasure my "aloneness." I never knew the joy of quietude and introspection, of pondering. (I had kept my life so busy and full, so noisy with life.) I felt the quiet overwhelming peace of the Spirit and the love of Heavenly Father and the Savior for me. He walked with me, and at times, I know He carried me. He wept with me. He ached with me. He warmed and healed me. As I turned my wretched worthless life over to Him, in willingness He carried me. He healed me with miracle upon miracle. Often it was through others and through nature. Finally, my eyes could see and I was no longer blind!

He helped me see my divine nature as His daughter and my great individual worth in His eyes. This worth, which brings me the inner joy I desired, is not based on the world's standards, but on my relationship with the Lord. His opinion should be the only one that matters. However, my earlier path had lead me down the road of narcissism, Satan's counterfeit to the Lord's plan. I did not realize how subtly I had skewed the Lord's teachings and what mistruths had resulted in my core belief windows.

I was lost, and now I am found. The peace I had been seeking all my life is now mine. That peace is independent of having a mate, of being a mother, of earning worldly accolades. That peace is grounded in my worth to my Heavenly

Father, in realizing my divine nature, and in knowing without doubt that He loves me despite my weaknesses.

I feel so blessed to have an opportunity to really lead a full life now. I do miss the companionship of an eternal mate, and it hangs me up at times. I have learned that the rapidly spiraling pity party can be stopped dead in its tracks by two actions. The first is by being thankful for anything and everything. Taking a walk and alerting my senses to all my surroundings gives me a quick jump-start at my list of things to be grateful for. That attitude is contagious and multiplies. The second quick step is to get outside of yourself and serve someone whose head and hands hang heavy. Heavenly Father is always quick to help us find someone to help. Now I can be His angel sometimes, the miracle others have been in my life.

The feeling of fulfillment and joy that comes from choosing to accept and obey my Heavenly Father's plan in my life has resulted in a peace, satisfaction, and a self-love that is incredible. I was lost, but now I am found.

The world pushes us by its standards of happiness. Yet those standards will always leave us empty. Being alone has been my greatest blessing, for I was not truly left alone. Father and the Savior entered my life, because I finally invited Them in to stay.

Healing from my silenced childhood pains, forgiving myself and my spouse, believing in myself, and truly being able to love and be loved have been rewards of this aloneness. Mortality has now opened up to me and now I am happy to be alive. I feel free to grow and learn forever!

Was it worth it? Yes, undoubtedly. I will never wish upon anyone that they learn these life lessons through divorce. But, if you find yourself single, please come to know that you are not alone. Your silent partners can come to walk with you 100% of the time, if you choose to let them. Heavenly Father, the Savior, and the companionship of the Holy Ghost will see you through to a place you could not imagine. They will be there to help you up when you fall and can't get up on your own and to carry you when you can no longer walk.

You are not alone. You can love and be loved more fully than you have ever known. I am still learning how to love and be loved. I am learning to nurture and love who I am. It is exhilarating, fulfilling, and risky, but so worthwhile and filling. I have joined the living! Yay! I know my family and friends have benefited too, as I am learning the pure love of Christ, also called charity. My heart has been softened and changed. I hope this process never ends. My heart is now full.

Please take courage and let Him love you as His precious daughter or son. Let Him help you see and to be no more blind.

Editors' Take: There is no reason to be afraid of being alone, because you never will be alone. Your Savior is always with you. He loves you and desires the best for you.

"Out of difficulties grow miracles." (Jean de la Bruyere)

Chapter Sixteen

My Story

BY MICHAEL AGRELIUS

Editors' Note: Remember who you are, Whose you are, who you want to become and then you will probably be kinder to everyone important to you; and everyone you come in contact with will become important to you.

Castle

I'll build you a castle, will you let it stand?
Catch a moonbeam, and place it in your hand.
Nothing too exquisite, nothing terribly fine;
I did it for you, I give you what's mine.

Be kind to that castle, hold tight to that beam . . .
Waves will surely come, to challenge the dream.
I live in the castle, you hold me in your hand . . .
Be kind to this lover, I'm made out of sand.

—m. agrelius

I wrote that poem shortly after I met the girl who I was to marry for time and all eternity. I was in love. I wanted it to work. Don't we all want it to work?

I don't think anyone goes into marriage not wanting it to work, and not doing everything they think they can to make it work, especially when there are precious children involved. So, what happened that twenty years later I wrote this next poem?

The Game

The field looks so simplistic—alternating squares of black, white,
    black and white again.
One royal family looking across to another.
Soldiers of choice not fortune, choosing to play the game.

Pawns, like small children lead the way.
Pawns, like small children seem to get in the way.
Pawns and small children are too easily swept away.

These are prizes not pawns.
These are reasons to live.
These are pawns who will be queens.
This is a game that never ends.

I take your castle, you take my knights.
You are my castle, you are my nights.
We play the game. We play the game.

You take my castle, we lose our pawns.
My king has no queen, the bishop is gone.
It's your move.

—m. agrelius

I think a big part of what went wrong was that I was selfish, with my time, and with my compliments. I spent too much time worrying about my own feelings. I wasn't appreciative enough of her, of my children, or of the blessings we had in our lives. I didn't keep my focus on the Lord. In saying that, I don't mean I was "inactive." I was very active in church. I just wasn't as active in the gospel, or our family. I wasn't as active in our marriage as I should have been. It was "me" more than it was "we." I wanted to be right more than I wanted to be on the same side. The bottom line is that I was seeking my own will rather than asking what Heavenly Father's will was for me and for us.

As you can probably see, *castles* were a significant metaphor in our courtship. I have since come to understand that many women appreciate that metaphor. Perhaps it is because castles are where you usually find princesses and because castles often symbolize security, loyalty, and a sense of safety, all traits that many women inherently seek. Of course, strong castles can sometimes feel cold, lonely, and even empty. That is the double-edged sword of metaphors.

The wedding was planned maybe more than we planned the marriage (at least that's how it seemed to me). We chose the Los Angeles Temple to get married in. Interestingly, temples can be seen as spiritual castles; only these castles are warm inside, eternal, and far from empty.

Sadly, after we got married I became focused on what I thought was a righteous desire, to get my career and our lives more established; I was also driven to get a house. I wanted to give her more of the temporal things in life and the world instead of nurturing her and our relationship. Unfortunately for me the temple became more like any another church activity or assignment instead of the place of eternal connections, energy, and love.

We both had testimonies of the gospel. I knew she was a good person and so I didn't figure we would ever get divorced regardless of what kind of challenges we had helped to create in our marriage. I wanted to do whatever I could to change, to make it right, and to keep it together. I'm sure pride was a major factor in why I didn't progress faster and more completely. I read President Benson's conference address on the subject at least eight or nine times and got something wonderful out of it each time I read it (see President Ezra Taft Benson, April 1989 general conference, "Beware of Pride"). It may be time for me to read it again.

We received counseling. I wanted to do whatever I could to change. I thought I had made progress. Maybe I did, but it apparently still wasn't enough. We got divorced twenty-one years after we met. And the confusing thing for me was that the problems began to surface at the exact time in life when I thought things were good. They arose when my temporal life was going good. We had a family, a home, some money in the bank, an established career, wonderful church callings, friends in the Church. It really looked to me like it was time to cruise into the home stretch. Those sentiments may have been part of the problem, too. I may have waited too long to shift my focus to things spiritual instead of measuring success by the things of this world. I have since come to understand that Heavenly Father's pattern is exactly opposite of what mine had been. He focuses on the spiritual first and then worries about the temporal or physical later (see D&C 29:30–35).

Divorce was the hardest thing I have ever done. It cut to my very spirit. Confidence turned to feelings of failure, insecurity, not being good enough, reviewing what went wrong until it made me depressed and hurting all over. If you've been divorced, or are contemplating it, then I don't need to tell you. It was the most soul-searching period in my life. I didn't know I had the capacity to pray that much or cry that much. I did, however, find comfort in the scriptures, in quotes from wonderful church leaders, and in the loving arms of the Comforter.

In the months prior to my divorce, and for many months after, I did a lot of kneeling down, a lot of asking, and a lot of pleading with Heavenly Father. I felt very much alone for quite a bit of the time during the marriage, and in fact thought of starting to write this book two years before we divorced, when I first realized we had serious problems in the marriage. My life has been on an emotional and spiritual roller coaster ever since.

In his visitation of the Father and the Son, the Prophet Joseph recorded, "Finding myself alone, I kneeled down and began to offer up the desire of my heart to God" (Joseph Smith—History 1:15). This quotation speaks volumes about how to prepare for and how to receive revelation. "Finding myself alone" is often when, where, and how we truly "find" ourselves, away from the crowd or even alone in the crowd.

Revelation often comes when we are alone, *and after* we "offer up the desire of our heart to God."

I've noticed another parallel with Joseph Smith's story and with the struggles of single life. Immediately after finding himself alone, a terrible darkness overcame Joseph. He said, "it seemed to me for a time as if I were doomed to sudden destruction" (Joseph Smith—History 1:32). Joseph had to persevere before he got his revelation.

For me, and many others, that pattern holds true in struggles with the darkness and despair of loneliness. Sometimes we feel as if we are doomed to destruction. But if we hang in there we can realize great blessings.

Approaching a Dream

Quietly edging up on my dream, my goal, my purpose.
  The rest of the world continues in its own endeavors, not noticing.
    And I'm kind of glad.

I've run over mountains and valleys, that I might walk this last mile.
  I've cried nights unnumbered, that I might be able to smile this
  one shining morning.
    I've looked with myself, that I might more fully know the universe.
      I've asked so many questions, so I might have this one assurance.
      Stayed awake in this real world, that I might have this one dream.

    And suddenly, here it comes, like light across the water, it dances
    on reflections of everything that I ever held as beautiful.

It softly reaches out to me, beckoning my common touch, and
with shaky hands, I hold that which is holy, just as I have been
held by hands made steady.

And now I walk on mirrors of kindness, truth and power, yet
still I run

    toward my final desire.

—m. agrelius

As I find myself alone, and I find myself offering up the
desire of my heart to God, I have been fortunate to receive
some revelations and impressions concerning my particular
situation. These have come to me over the course of several years in response to much prayer, but usually not as the
answer I was expecting. For example, early in my struggles I
was told quite plainly in my heart, "You are a son of God."
The strange thing was that I was praying about something
completely different. I think I was asking what I needed to
do in order to help things to work out in my marriage, so we
wouldn't have to go through with the divorce.

I think my initial reaction was, "That's great to know
that I am your son, but not what I was asking for." However,
I have since reflected on it many times, and it is very comforting to have the knowledge that no matter what happens I
am a child of a loving, constant, kind, and accepting Father
in Heaven. That knowledge was especially comforting later
when we actually got divorced, helping me to understand
in some small measure how the Only Begotten Son of God
asked not to drink the bitter cup. Rather than seek His own
will, He sought the will of His Father. He passed through

the pain and anguish in Gethsemane and on the cross, alone, so that He could fulfill His mission that we might have the opportunity for eternal life. I didn't like the cup that was before me either, much as I am sure that Joseph Smith was not thrilled with his months in Liberty Jail, and much like I assume you weren't looking forward to what was, or is, before you.

A kind bishop pointed out a comforting scripture to me during one of my toughest times:

> *Ye cannot behold with your natural eyes, for the present time, the design of your God concerning those things which shall come hereafter, and the glory which shall follow after much tribulation.*
>
> *For after much tribulation come the blessings. Wherefore the day cometh that ye shall be crowned with much glory; the hour is not yet, but is nigh at hand.*
>
> *Remember this, which I tell you before, that you may lay it to heart, and receive that which is to follow."* (*D&C 58:3–5*)

Out of my trial came my discovery and the positive insight that I am a son of God. I also know that my former spouse is a daughter of God and deserves to be treated with godly respect by virtue of her divine lineage. I further realize that everyone who is in a similar situation to me is a son or daughter of God and that those who they were married to are also children of that same loving Father.

Freedom's Fairest Skies

Freedom's fairest skies call to you and me,
  With freshness and with life, come explore eternity.
Pure, untouched and clean, a new horizon found;
  Can your heart and soul contain the beautifully gentle sound?

Time is now gone, and no longer of concern.
  The only measures binding are those for which we yearn.
The heavens now unfold, brighter than the brightest sun;
  Light shed upon the past, from Deity we've come.

The knowledge of the mysteries, more glorious than the stars,
  The power of the universe now is part of ours.
To travel far beyond, and yet within the spaces.
  We've surpassed our earthly limits to dwell in exalted places.

And life shall never end; nor light nor love nor we,
  We're learning all the time, what makes the skies so free.

—m. agrelius

Editors' Take: The Lord's pattern is spiritual first and then temporal. That being said, it appears that being alone can be very conducive to receiving revelation, and sometimes necessary to fulfilling our mission here in life.

"The Spirit itself beareth witness with our spirit, that we are the children of God: And if children, then heirs; heirs of God, and joint-heirs with Christ; if so be that we suffer with him, that we may be also glorified together. For I reckon that the sufferings of this present time are not worthy to be compared with the glory which shall be revealed in us." (Romans 8:16–18)

Chapter Seventeen

The Eternal Value of a Stamp and a Get-Well Card

BY CLAUDIA

Editors' Note: Harboring ill feelings toward anyone isn't healthy.

The best thing about personal growth is when it happens, it is oh so noticeable. It may take a while, but when it happens, it shines through clear as daybreak.

When I got divorced after ten years of marriage, I could tell you every rotten thing my husband ever did to me, forgetting what I might have done to him. Neither of us had any conflict resolution skills so getting a divorce was the easy thing to do.

After the divorce, I continued to live a single's life that made me happy, doing what I wanted to do, when I wanted, being accountable to no one but my children and me, eating banana splits for supper when we felt like it, taking off at the drop of a hat, packing up my children and going where

103

we wanted when we wanted. It was not a bad life, not bad at all. The children grew up to have successful happy lives. Forgetting what the Lord has counseled on eternal marriage, I continued to live my "me" and "I" life.

It took twenty years for me to understand that it indeed must take "two to tango," and in order to go on to the future, you must make amends with the past. That's why second marriages fail faster than first ones, because people haven't been able to do that.

So, twenty years quickly disappeared since my divorce. Recently, and at the same time, almost exactly to the day, my ex and I both came down with illnesses. Our daughter kept us both posted on things like that, since we live far away from each other and have no reason to communicate— heck, we couldn't when we lived together, why bother when there are twelve states between us and a grown daughter?

When my ex found out I was having health issues, he sent me a get-well card, and a nice letter telling me he hoped I would soon be well, and told me a little bit about his illness. This kind gesture took my breath away, since we had no contact with each other for twelve years since my daughter's wedding. And all verbal and written communications prior to that had not been pleasant. All those years of feeling bitterness can't be good for anyone. It surely wasn't for me. He had his own struggles also, having a second failed marriage in that time. (I have remained single.)

So, after I read the card, I sent him a nice email hoping he would recover soon, his illness being much more serious in nature than mine. I was so grateful he had a new wife that loved him and took good care of him. I put his name on the prayer roll at the Mount Timpanogos Utah Temple on several occasions over the coming year, and the peace I felt was indescribable. It is impossible for me to put these feelings into adequate words, so suffice it to say that it is a feeling I will never forget.

Suddenly all of the bitterness I felt all these years flew out the window, and all it took was a get-well card and a postage stamp.

For those of you who are struggling with divorce, don't carry your anger and resentment and pitiful feelings around like some sort of badge and make it the subject of all your conversations. Make peace with your ex so that you are able to heal from your wounds. Do now what it has taken me twenty years to do. Who knows, maybe you may just choose your ex as a friend, if not for now, then in the eternities when we are all a bit more perfected.

The scriptures that sound so wonderful to me at this time in my life are

In my Father's house are many mansions: if it were not so, I would have told you. I go to prepare a place for you. (John 14:2)

Let not your hearts be troubled; for in my Father's house are many mansions, and I have prepared a place for you; and where my Father and I am, there ye shall be also. (D&C 98:18)

In order to inherit these promises someday, we must be free of ill feelings toward others, including all bitterness and anger. The Lord will help us, but it is truly our choice to own it. Now that I have forgiven, I am ready to live many more years on this earth, and, if the hoped-for opportunity finally presents itself, marry.

Editors' Take: Forgiveness and kindness are the higher ground that can give us a glimpse of heaven.

"Happiness is the object and design of our existence, and will be the end thereof if we pursue the path that leads to it; and this path is virtue, uprightness, faithfulness, holiness, and keeping all of the commandments of God." (Joseph Smith)

Chapter Eighteen

Prince in Training

BY JOHN CANAAN

Editors' Note: Being "alone" gives us opportunities and choices. One of the opportunities is to face ourselves, our former spouse, and God with honesty and without guile.

Here's the big thing for me: Divorce has given me a choice between two things. First, I could choose to go deeper into the very denial and blame that contributed to the divorce in the first place. Or instead, to come clean about everything that I contributed to create my divorce, or in other words, everything I have held back from my former wife and ultimately from God.

I think of the man in the New Testament who came to Peter, having held back a part of his property from the United Order of that time. That man, having held back, dropped dead at the feet of Peter (Acts 5:1–10). What a symbol. Holding back what I really needed to come completely forward with caused my marriage to "drop dead" in a sense.

I can either seek to look at all the ways I held back all the things that I didn't give 100% on, or I can figure out a way to explain it all as my former wife's fault, arguing that "if she would have just done this or if she wouldn't have done that" everything would have been fine.

But if I am tempted to blame, I think of another story from the New Testament in Luke 18:11–14, that I'll modify slightly to make a point. "A Pharisee stood in the temple and praying within himself, said, essentially, 'Lord I'm thankful that I'm not as other men are.' A publican, there in the same moment, would not so much lift his eyes unto Heaven, but striking his hand upon his breast said, 'God be merciful unto *me* [not my wife, but unto *me*] a sinner.' Verily, verily I say unto you, this man went down to his house justified—or, I might add, happy."

There is a great happiness that has come to me in trying to see as clearly as I can what I contributed to my divorce. This is not to say that my former wife didn't contribute something. But I cannot repent of her shortcomings. In fact, I'm not sure if I even *care* about her shortcomings. I *can* repent of my sins though. And I can believe that, as I do repent, through the Atonement of Christ I will be forgiven and made whole and be worthy to stand before Him one day and hear Him say "Well done my good and faithful servant."

Repenting is not self-punishment. It is self-liberation. Self-punishment is when we don't believe in Christ's love for us and His ability and willingness to lift us and forgive us. When we don't believe in this, then we certainly must punish *ourselves* enough to feel forgiven. But life is punishing enough. I would rather repent, believe in Christ, and keep repenting. What else is there?

So that is what I've continued to do. And each day I find a new layer of something I am holding back from the ones I love, and in this sense, from God. It is painful to look hard at myself. But it is liberating to change. And it is a liberation that opens to me, hopefully, a future that will be different from my past.

I will share a moment that still warms my heart to think about.

Sometime after our divorce, I recorded a song called "I Am Your Prince," originally written for a couple's wedding (a second marriage for both). Ultimately, though, as I thought of what my former wife really needed from me, and what I had held back, the song ended up being dedicated to her, an effort to heal some of her wounds, even though the divorce had long since been finalized and my former wife was very happily involved with someone else.

I remember taking the recording to her and sitting on the ground to listen to it with her. There was something about the way Sam Cardon had recorded it that truly caught the spirit of how healing it is for someone to really come through for them. So, she and I sat there on the ground and just cried our eyes out. Because it was then that she knew that I knew what the song meant, and how much she had needed me to sing it to her throughout our marriage. I'm not saying that I didn't also need her to sing it to me. I *am* saying that the more I understand and, through the grace of God, work on what needs to change in me, the more I feel able to sing this song and the happier I feel.

> *Once the little girl in you, sat alone and cried,*
> *Looked into the sky above—and wondered when her prince*
>   *would come*
> *Someone who would lift her, and tell her she was beautiful.*
> *Now the days have come and gone and all that could of has*
>   *gone wrong.*
> *You have left this dream behind.*
> *And you have kissed your prince good night.*
> *But look at me with open eyes.*
> *I'm the one you dreamed of.*
> *I am your prince.*
> *I am the one you saw, up in the sky above.*
> *And I can reach through the years by loving you as you are.*
>
> *Once a little girl like you had a childhood dream come true*
> *And found her way to someone's heart who loved her as she was.*
> *I am your prince.*
> *I am the one you saw up in the sky above.*
> *And I can reach through the tears by loving you as you are.*
> *And I love you for who you are.*
>
> —*John Canaan*

Editors' Take: Being honest gives us opportunities to realize the best in us, and when we do that we also realize and bring out the best in others.

"You can clutch the past so tightly to your chest that it leaves your arms too full to embrace the present." (Jane Glidwell)

Chapter Nineteen

The Value of Divorce

BY MR. A. NONOMUS

Editors' Note: Being Christlike is not limited, and often not convenient.

While divorce is not uplifting and is not often a display of kindness and Christlike actions, it is valuable. I have grown spiritually from the event. I guess we have an opportunity in divorce to choose either to be ugly or to be kind, forgiving, and respectful. It is hard to do the latter, but the value of the latter is that in a very difficult situation we are doing what is right.

I know that my tendency when the separation occurred (which I was not expecting) was to be distraught, fearful, angry, and to some extent puzzled. As I determined what I would do, I considered that life was not worth anything, life in the Church did not make sense, living the commandments was too hard under the circumstances, and the gospel must not be true.

It took some time to work through my issues, and the only way I made it through was to attend the temple and ask Heavenly Father for help. He gave me help line upon line, bit by bit, and I survived and am healthier now than I was before the divorce. Yes, the divorce was wrong and unnecessary, but the results were, in my case, good, because I made changes in my life that I would not have made otherwise.

Essentially, I was forced to evolve. I knew that if I became angry, I would lose my way and ultimately lose my testimony. So I fasted and prayed to receive help in strengthening my weaknesses. I found courage, strength, and patience, not to mention a release for anger, lust, and fear.

The anger was the first to go. I had to let it go, or it would spiritually eat me alive. Then I gave up lust. Being married, you have physical relations and when single, you must either give it up or lose your temple recommend and ultimately your membership. I could not live with those consequences, so I gave up the lust. First, I gave up the action, or I was forced to give it up. Then I gave up the thought. Thought was much harder since I had memories that were difficult to erase. Then, after a year, I was able to give up the desire. I felt like I was losing a part of myself as I let it go, but there was a reward: the Spirit was stronger and I was much happier. As it says in the Book of Mormon, we must bridle all our passions that we may have love in our hearts. I learned that removing the desire allowed the love for others to be stronger. It took some time, but ultimately there was peace and great joy.

Finally, I had to give up fear. I am still working on this. I had fear that I would not get to see the children. I had fear that I would not find an eternal companion. I had fear of leaving the Church. I gradually overcame most of them and replaced them with the peace that Heavenly Father offers. The peace comes from accepting His will and not worrying about the arm of flesh. By letting go of my fears, I felt His comfort. This was not an event. It came and went. Gradually, I could function without the fear and if it came, I could quickly push it away.

As I processed the situation, I found myself relying on a Neal A. Maxwell quote, which states, "Heavenly Father is looking for a change in character, not a change in circumstance." So I worked at understanding what characteristics needed work and I pursued them.

It is hard work making oneself different. However, it is worth it. I would not go back to my former self, even if I would have my family situation restored. I could not go through the pain again. I do not want to be like I was. I guess it just goes to show that Heavenly Father knows what He is doing when He allows us to be tested. We evolve and change either for the better or for the worse. It is our choice. And if we do not evolve for the better, we will likely face the same situation again, just different and worse. This is the reason that I do not want to go backwards.

I feel I am much better prepared to face bigger challenges. As a tree is strengthened by the wind, so I was strengthened by divorce.

Editors' Take: Being Christlike is the ultimate goal for us in this life. Making the sacrifices and striving to attain that goal prepares us for everything else in this life and the next.

"Have patience with everything unresolved in your heart and try to love the questions themselves as if they were locked rooms or books written in a very foreign language. Don't search for the answers, which could not be given you now, because you would not be able to live them. And the point is, to live everything. Live the questions now. Perhaps then, someday far in the future, you will gradually, without ever noticing it, live your way into the answer." (Rainer Maria Rilke)

Chapter Twenty

Fifteen Push-Ups

BY KATHRYN K. DURRANT

Editors' Note: Daily we have options before us. Victories come to us through small and large accomplishments.

On a recent flight I sat next to a boy who looked to be about six years old. He was traveling alone so I struck up a conversation. When we were high over the mountains he suddenly asked me what would happen if we crashed. In an effort to ease his fears I replied, "We'll gather sticks and branches and make a hut where we can sleep. Then we'll look for nuts and berries to eat and maybe find a stream for a drink of water." He looked me in the eye and replied, "I'd rather be dead."

He didn't like the option I presented. We don't always like the options presented to us when our lives come crashing down. How do we press forward then, with a steadfast faith in Christ (see 2 Nephi 31:20)? How do we press forward when our dreams seem to have been taken away? How do we keep hope's flame burning bright?

I'm divorced. At the time I got divorced I had very little education. Over time I was able to complete my associate's degree and then my bachelor's degree. I graduated alongside my oldest daughter. I then worked two years before I felt prompted to take the LSAT, a test taken by those who want to attend law school. I am pleased to say I knew what the LSAT was. I just didn't realize people studied for months before taking it. My first indication of this came when I went to the testing site and found hundreds of people, anxious people, there to take the test.

The prompting to take the LSAT came as I walked my two dogs one fall evening. I would walk them around my block each night at ten o'clock and then go to bed. I was the Primary chorister at the time so as I walked I would sing whatever song I was teaching the children. On this night it was "Press Forward, Saints," which I began singing at a spot where the road gently sloped. As the road leveled out I reached the song's end, bursting into the chorus of "hallelujah, hallelujah, hallelujah." It was then I felt the prompting that I should take the LSAT. I thought God's prompting was nicely choreographed.

It had never been my goal to become a lawyer, so after the test was over I did nothing about applying to schools. I just knew I was supposed to take the test. I remember thinking, *There, I did what you asked.* A year later I realized, yes, I was also supposed to also apply to law schools. I began that process and I'm proud to say I got into every school to which

I applied. Sounds impressive yes, but I only applied to two. When I would tell people I was in law school at Brigham Young University I often got the response, "I thought that was hard to get into?" Hum, how do you answer that?

Three very difficult and rewarding years later, and a topic for another day, I graduated. I put a quote on my graduation announcements. It was a quote I'd seen while ordering transcripts for my law school applications. I'd liked it so I had quickly written it down on the backside of a transcript request form. For three years it hung on my bathroom mirror. It read, "While we may not know in the beginning what the exact results of our effort may be . . . we can know with almost certainty what they will be if we chose to do nothing."

I had chosen to do something. I certainly did not know in the beginning how my life would change from following a small prompting to take the LSAT, but I did know it would be better than choosing nothing. For several years after my divorce the theme of my life came from the song "I Dreamed a Dream" from the musical *Les Miserables*. "I always dreamed my life would be, so different from this hell I'm living." Now instead of just dreaming for better things, I was taking action.

The LSAT and law school weren't the first actions I'd ever taken. I started out small. I wanted something different and that required an effort. I wanted to have "Hope's bright flame" in my life as 2 Nephi 31:20 alludes to and the hymn "Press Forward, Saints" states. I learned that hope is not a wish, but rather it is a confident expectation. After taking a law school final I was confident I would pass. Not with the best marks, but I'd pass. I had worked hard and I knew I was where I was supposed to be. I had the hope of a future in the law and I was confident I would succeed.

When I graduated from law school, I got a clerkship in the Fourth District Court. This was not a regular clerkship. I would also be the bailiff. This meant I would wear a uniform and have handcuffs, pepper spray, and a baton to enforce the law if anyone didn't obey the court's rules. In order to qualify for this I had to be trained. I had to attend Police Officer Standards Training, or POST. When I was finished, I would be a special functions officer. The training would last almost six weeks.

POST has physical fitness requirements. This would be for my safety and for the public's safety. I've never been very athletic so I started several months before POST to get in shape. I began running. I'd have to run a mile and a half in under sixteen minutes. I worked on sit-ups; thirty would be required in under a minute. I also did exercises to strengthen my upper body so I could do the required fifteen push-ups. It was not easy. I worked very hard at it.

During POST we had physical training, which included running and exercise, and we learned defensive tactics. I pushed myself more physically and mentally than I ever had in my whole life. Some days I'd come home and lie on my bed and cry out of sheer exhaustion. I wanted this job and it was killing me. Our class was the 236th class to attend POST. Our motto became "236 no one quits" and I didn't want to be a quitter. As hard as it was, I had hope, that confident expectation, that I could do this.

At the beginning of POST we'd done a physical test in the three areas and I had failed each one, even with my months of work. Now the final day had come for our physical test. I did my thirty sit-ups in the required time, but my push-ups were unsuccessful. I had promised myself that I would not cry during POST, but after my push-ups I went out in the hall and the tears flowed. I hadn't succeeded; all my months of effort and I had failed.

Word came from Bobbi, a friend I had made during POST training, that I could have another chance at the push-ups on another day. Bobbi was a woman who was only a few years younger than me, but unlike me she was in great physical shape. I knew I had to make this run in less than sixteen minutes. I didn't want to ever run it again. I donned a visor from Bobbi. She'd soaked it in water to help keep me cool. I checked the pace watch my sister had loaned me and took off with the group; quickly I became the lone runner at the end of the pack.

I knew the pace I had to maintain to finish in less than sixteen minutes. I ran steadily, checking my watch frequently. The course was set up so that we ran up to a certain point and then ran back to the finish. Soon runners sprinted past me going the other direction, encouragements wafting to me over their shoulders as they sped by. I got to the turn around and the officer standing there encouraged me with a gruff, "You're going to have to pick it up or you'll never make it." I checked my special watch. I could do it but I couldn't slow down. It was a miserable hot day. All I could think was I have to make it and how good it would feel to just quit running and sit down right where I was. I'd already failed the push-ups.

From a bend in the path, I saw Bobbi running towards me. Bobbi had promised she'd run me in. When we'd go running for physical training, the first people finished would turn around, run back, and pick up the stragglers and run in with them, or to be more precise, run in with me. They would run alongside me and encourage me. I'd get a burst of energy and sprint to the finish. Then we'd all gather around and cheer, "236 no one quits."

Bobbi had promised, "I'll come back for you and run you in." At the sight of her, I knew I was almost there. She got to me and encouraged me as we ran, her just a step ahead, willing me to go a little faster. Others joined us in the run, all shouting encouragements. I pushed harder and crossed the line with a time of 15:45. I sat down in exhaustion, thrilled by my accomplishment, surrounded by well-wishers offering pats on the back and congratulations. We all gathered in a sweaty circle and yelled "236 no one quits!"

Have hope that others will be there for you and at the same time, be there for others. I had never played sports so I didn't realize the bond that could form when a group went through difficult things together. I don't think any of those people realized how close I was to quitting each day. We also don't know how close to quitting the people around us might be at any given time. So in our own lives, let's remember to turn around, go back, and help those who aren't as far ahead in this single life as some of us are, giving them encouragement. Let's remember that Christ is also always right at our side, wanting us to make it. Let's make sure no one quits. Let's help each other to succeed.

POST was done. I now had to study for the bar. I wanted to quickly complete the push-up requirement and focus on my studies. In my effort to do this, I overexerted myself and became injured. Due to this injury and my recovery, I had to begin again. I started over with no push-ups to my credit. I hired a personal trainer and she carefully led me through exercises that allowed me to get strong in a safe manner. I was allowed to begin my clerkship but I couldn't wear my uniform until I had completed the push-up requirement.

After several months, I felt I was ready. I scheduled an appointment with the officer at the jail who had authority to pass me off. At POST we called him Magnum P.I. because he looked just like the TV character. I put on what looked like a 7th grade gym outfit and headed out to do fifteen push-ups in front of the best-looking sheriff in the county. I began. Slowly and methodically, I went up and down until he called out fourteen, but I could not come back up on what would have been my fifteenth push-up.

I was stunned. I had failed again. All my effort was still not enough. I tried to hold the tears back but I could not. I lay there on the jail floor and cried. Poor Magnum P.I.; he was saying encouraging words but it didn't soothe me. As I left he assured me he'd be willing to watch me try again any time and as many times as it would take.

Two weeks later, I was back. I got down into push-up position and he began to count. He got to thirteen, fourteen, and then said, "That's fifteen," but I kept on going until I reached twenty. Then I got up and let the celebration burst out. I jumped around the room cheering and clapping. I thanked him and went leaping and running out of the jail. I had done it. It had taken me four months but I had done it. "236 no one quits."

I have a sign that hangs in my office "If we wait for the moment when everything, absolutely everything, is ready, we shall never begin" (Ivan Turgenev). It helps me to dive in and start new things. I also know that even if you are on the right track in life, you can't sit down. Alma 34:41 tells us to have a "firm hope" and 1 Peter 1:3 says to have a "lively hope." Hope needs to be a bright flame burning as we do things with a confident expectation that we will achieve our goal of eternal life.

I've related two major accomplishments in my life, law school and POST, but most of our lives are made up of small accomplishments. I'll now tell you of two small accomplishments in my life. First, I make my bed every day. I didn't always do this. Then I read that people who make their beds in the morning have more order in their life, which makes them more attractive. I wanted more order in my life and I wanted to be more attractive. It was worth a shot. I started with a small thing, but I have hope, a confident expectation, that one day an organized closet will result and I will be more attractive.

The other small accomplishment is each morning I read a page, front and back, of scriptures before I get out of bed. I turn on the light, turn off the alarm, and read. I have learned that once I get going on the day the time for scriptures seems to slip away. So when I heard the challenge to the Young Women to read their scriptures daily, I decided I was young enough to join in. I already prayed and smiled daily, but my daily scripture reading was spotty. I know that this small accomplishment will grow into something great.

With these big and little accomplishments, I was growing in my testimony of hope. When I hoped for things with a confident expectation, which means to include the Lord when you jump to action, things happened. I had faith that this was true. I was ready for the big one.

I wanted to marry again, so I took it to the Lord and told Him of my desire and asked what I could do so I would be ready to marry again if that opportunity came to me. His answer was to work on my family. Not what I had expected, but my family relationships during law school had suffered. Not just the relationship between my children and me, but also my children's relationships with each other.

As I pondered the Lord's answer, ideas began to come. I then implemented them. I didn't wait. I talked to my two sons who worked downtown, like I did, and we picked Tuesday as a day we could all get together for lunch. Each Tuesday we went to a different restaurant and ate, talked, reviewed the food, laughed, and went back to work. The girls were not to be left out. My daughter, Emma; her daughter Emery; and my daughter in-laws, Kelly and Nicole, would join me once a month for girl's night. We watched movies, had pedicures, went on shopping trips, and in the end participated in a Woman's Walk in Boise, Idaho, where my oldest daughter, Katie, lives.

I wrote a family letter and mailed it. (It is so nice to get a letter in the mail instead of a bill!) I'd take the news I'd learned from my lunch with the boys, talk to my daughters, throw in some news from the extended family, and ship the letter out. Now they all knew what was going on in each of their lives so they could talk to each other. It took more time and money than an e-mail, but it was time and money well spent.

We began to have Sunday Night Scones on the first Sunday of the month. No one was ever expected to come, but it was offered. We usually had everyone there; how could they resist hot scones?

Lastly, we planned a reunion. I knew my job would end in July so in January we picked the first weekend of August. I put down the deposit on a house at Lava Hot Springs, Idaho, central to all of us. I announced it. I promoted it in the letter. I divided out cooking and cleaning assignments. I bought bright orange towels (very lava like) and had a good friend embroider every person's name on their very own towel. The reunion was the cherry on top of all my efforts to bring my family close together.

I returned on Wednesday from that great time with my family only to get a phone call on Thursday offering me a job in New Mexico. I was so grateful that I had done what I had done for and with my family. Now I could move away confident that they were closer to each other and that family bonds had been strengthened.

I still have problems; my family still has problems. Problems don't go away. I'm still not married even though I make my bed. I probably have more problems now, but I have been strengthened in them. Years ago, in what I call my bleak period, my daughter gave me this quote, which I didn't like at the time but I hung on the refrigerator anyway, hoping one day I'd learn to be reconciled to what the Lord had for me and know it was for my good:

> *We have not had one day of good sailing in a month; it is either calms or light head winds. We seldom sail more than from thirty to fifty miles in twenty-four hours. We are hungry, and weary, and lonesome, and disconsolate. But, after praying much for a fair wind and speed, we find our prayers are not answered, and we have given it up, and have asked our Heavenly Father to give us patience and reconciliation to His will.* (Parley P. Pratt)

In court we schedule trials dates, but in life we don't have that luxury. It always struck me as funny when I work at the court to say, "I've got a trial today." In life we could say that every morning as we wake up. Trials will come, but with steadfast faith in Christ, with a bright flame of hope to light the way, we can press forward. Press forward even though we may not be able to see too far in front.

One of the last songs I taught the children as ward Primary chorister before I moved to New Mexico was "How

Firm a Foundation." When I taught the third verse, I put the words up and said to the children. "Who is saying this?" Then I put up a picture of Jesus. We then sang, "Fear not, I am with thee; oh be not dismayed, for I am thy God and will still give thee aid. I'll strengthen thee, bless thee, and cause thee to stand, upheld by my righteous omnipotent hand."

Through small things and large things, I know I am not alone in this journey. I have found hope and I am enduring to the end.

Editors' Take: Reflecting on our victories and accomplishments make us better prepared to press forward.

"How many truly great individuals do you know who never struggled?" (Joe J. Christensen)

Chapter Twenty-One

Christ's Atonement and the Single Life

By Michael Agrelius

Editors' Note: Pain, sorrow, and being single allows us to relate in part to just some of what the Savior experienced for us so we can return to our Heavenly Home.

A number of years ago I was visiting my brother at his place and did something very dumb. Okay, that's not so unusual, since I often do dumb things when I get together with either of my brothers. But this time the dumb thing really hurt. I lifted a bed from the floor and while I was lifting, I twisted at the same time. The result was that I threw my back out. Over the course of the next few hours, I got more and more crooked and I experienced greater and greater pain. Within a day or so, I couldn't stand it any longer and I decided I needed serious help.

I made an appointment and drove myself downtown to a chiropractor's office. I struggled to get out of the car, pounding my hand on the top of my car trying to get the attention of anyone because I couldn't even take a step without crying in pain. I remember thinking at that time what a privilege it was to be able to receive just a very small glimpse of the pain that I imagine the Savior felt in the Garden of Gethsemane. I'm guessing that many women have similar feelings about that closeness with the Savior during childbirth.

That was years ago, but I am occasionally reminded of that experience when my back "goes out."

Recently, I was reading a wonderful book called *The Infinite Atonement* when I came across this passage:

> *The Savior's descent to humanity was personally announced by the Savior to Nephi on the first "Christmas Eve". "Behold. The time is at hand . . . on the morrow come I into the world" (3 Nephi 1:13). Oh, the magnitude of that sacrifice, that condescension! That night, God the Son traded his heavenly home with all its celestial adornments for a mortal abode with all its primitive trappings. He, "the King of heaven" (Alma 5:50), "the Lord Omnipotent who reigneth" (Mosiah 3:5), left a throne to inherit a manger. He exchanged the dominion of a god for the dependence of a babe. He gave up wealth, power, dominion, and the fullness of his glory—for what?—for taunting, mocking, humiliation, and subjection. It was a trade of unparalleled dimension, a condescension of incredible proportions,*

a descent of incalculable depth. (Tad R. Callister, *The Infinite Atonement*, pp. 63–64)

While I am in no way attempting to assume a total understanding of Christ's Atonement, I think that many of us who are divorced, many who are widowed, and many who have yet to marry but who have known the joys of a good family, receive a small glimpse of what it is like to give up wealth, comfort, a fullness of family, even glory if you will, for the often perceived humiliation, subjection, and trappings of something so primitive and terrestrial as the single life. We are privileged to relate a little more than we may have related with the Great Redeemer.

As painful as this single life sometimes is, it is good to know that we are not really alone, and that Someone much greater than us has descended further, and trodden a more seemingly impossible path in order to make our futures, even our eternities, brighter and more complete.

Thanks be to a heavenly family, our Heavenly Father and His Son, and to all the other support we feel from the seen and unseen world that give us courage when times are tough in this journey of life.

Editors' Note: The pain and trials we experience in this life help us better understand, and come closer to, the One who gave us eternal life.

"We do not always receive inspiration or revelation when we request it. Sometimes we are delayed in the receipt of revelation, and sometimes we are left to our own judgment. We cannot force spiritual things. It must be so. Our life's purpose to obtain experience and to develop faith would be frustrated if our Heavenly Father directed us in every act, even in every important act. We must make decisions and experience the consequences in order to develop self-reliance and faith." (Dallin H. Oaks)

Section Four

Thoughts, Insights & Discoveries for Those Who Have Been Widowed

I Can't Tell You

I can't tell you how long this storm will last
  You might not care even if I could
I can't tell you how hard the rain will fall
  It really doesn't matter—it's gonna fall no matter how hard it is
    and it will continue to fall until it's done
    and then it will fall again—that's just what rain does
I can't tell you when the sun will come out to warm your spirit
  I've wondered about it myself

All I know is—it will come

You will smile again in the sunshine
  Flowers will bloom in your backyard
Friends will come with joy and laughter
  You will dance on a moonlit night—with a touch of the sun
    still on your cheek
  The stars will hold you in their memories
Pictures will hang on your walls
And love will warm your soul again
    especially on cloudy days

—m. agrelius

Chapter Twenty-Two

Life Is Too Short

By Amy Day

Editors' Note: There is a time for sorrow and heartache, but the Lord wants to strengthen us and help us to overcome.

My husband passed away eighteen months ago. For me it feels like eighteen years. Every month that passes feels like a year. Even though it's been a short while I feel like I've been alone a long time. He was buried on our eighteenth wedding anniversary. I have five children, ages seventeen, fifteen, twelve, nine, and four. Each has had a monumental event occur in their lives where their dad wasn't there to participate.

My oldest turned sixteen, got his driver's license, was ordained a priest, and got his black belt. He baptized his younger brother when he turned eight, who became a cub scout, and played his first season in basketball. My middle child turned twelve, received the priesthood, and started middle school. His older brother was able to help set him apart to be a deacon. My oldest daughter turned fourteen, started high school, went to her first church dance, and played high school soccer. My youngest daughter started preschool and wonders where her daddy is. She thinks about him every day and worries because she's "starting to forget." We survived the first year but now realize there are many more years to survive. I'm not willing to just survive. I want to grab life and *live* it. I want my children to see that you can suffer great heartache and setbacks but you can come back stronger, smarter, and better.

"Verily, Verily, I say unto you, That ye shall weep and lament, but the world shall rejoice: and ye shall be sorrowful, but your sorrow shall be turned into joy." (John 16:20)

One day I felt the world crashing down on me. I felt weak and alone. But then I felt a surge of strength and I shook my fist, like Scarlett O'Hara, and shouted, "Bring it on. You think you're going to crush me? I can take whatever you got. I'm not going down." An inner strength I never realized I had emerged and made me stronger.

"Strengthened with all might, according to his glorious power, unto all patience and longsuffering with joyfulness." (Colossians 1:11)

My self-confidence has increased immensely since my husband's death. I know I have been blessed by prayers and by the Holy Spirit. But an element of self-reliance has busted out and energized me to succeed.

My husband may have died but I am very much alive and have several missions still on earth to complete.

"If thou art sorrowful, call on the Lord thy God with sup-plication, that your souls may be joyful." (D&C 136:29)

I liked being married. I liked having a friend and com-panion. I'm not willing to go through the rest of my life alone; life is too short. I know I can find love and happiness again. So is it okay to say you want to date? Are you disre-specting your deceased spouse? Will your children resent it? Will your in-laws criticize you?

Just like you always have room in your heart to love one more child, I believe I have room in my heart to love again. I'm okay with that and everyone who loves and cares about me is okay with that too. I asked my children how they felt about me starting to date. "Whatever makes you happy, Mom" was their response.

Progress is being made. I can walk through the mall and sometimes I forget I'm a widow. It's such an ugly word. Widows are little old ladies with white hair and lots of cats. I don't want to be a widow.

Actually, seeing the many widows after 9/11 gave me strength. I know I'm not alone. I'm not the only one this has happened to. I know I am being watched over and taken care of. I have faith that things will work out for me. I will take what I've been dealt and make the best out of a tough situ-ation. I will endure to the end and have joy in the journey.

"And ye now therefore have sorrow: but I will see you again, and your heart shall rejoice, and your joy no man taketh from you. And in that day ye shall ask me nothing [but it shall be done unto you—JST]. Verily, verily, I say unto you, Whatsoever ye shall ask the Father in my name, he will give it you. Hitherto

have ye asked nothing in my name: ask, and ye shall receive, that your joy may be full." (John 16:22–24)

Editors' Take: The Lord wants us to have joy and a fullness of life. That is not to say we can't grieve, but it is to say that He doesn't want us to stay in a constant state of grief. We should strive to endure to the end and have joy in the journey.

He is Your Friend

When the weight is on your shoulders
When your spirit cries within
Know He's there to share your burdens
Know He knows—He is your Friend

When you feel the pains and pressures
When you cringe to drink the cup
Know He's there to steady your hand
Know He's there to fill you up

When the world no longer makes sense . . .
And your hiding places are all gone
Know He's there to shield and comfort
Know He'll stay until the dawn

He is your Friend—He's here to save you
He knows your trials and your pain
He hears your prayers through your crying
He knows your heart and your name

—m. agrelius

Chapter Twenty-Three

I Shall Clasp Thee Again

BY S. MICHAEL WILCOX

Editors' Note: Widows will be reunited with their eternal companions but need not wish for death to come earlier than it may. When death does come it will bring with it the blessings of a renewed, perfected love.

Is death the enemy? Surely it brought the ache within my heart that will not, perhaps must not be abated, but that soreness of soul is becalmed by a sense of peace and gratitude. Peace that she is at peace, and gratitude that my feelings for her have intensified. These have been days of pain, the greatest I have ever known, but also of profound love. Nothing could possibly have shown me more than Laurie's losing battle with cancer how very much I love her and will always love her. That above all else has been made crystal clear. Death, as part of that great plan of happiness and mercy, intensifies our need for each other like nothing else can. And so I am grateful for its lessons, though the cost is so immeasurably high. To love at all is to expose the soul to the possibility of pain. Only in the blackest regions of outer darkness is there no love, and that is a torment of its own kind and making. Here our grief would go, but only if the love departed also, and who would be willing to escape suffering at that price? No, rather we would bear an increase in our anguish to feel, to know beyond all misgivings, hesitations, disbeliefs, and doubts, the joy of being loved and of loving.

Many times, like most of us with those dearest to us, I have taken Laurie for granted, did not tell her enough how much she meant to me because, though I loved her and expressed that love, I did not know myself how deep the roots had grown. Now there is no doubt, no reservation—all is certainty, pure confidence. I cannot find the space within where I could say, "Here is the dwelling place she does not touch, where her absence is not missed." I know—and I hope and believe that she now knows—how completely she dominates the soul and thoughts of her husband. She fills a place within that no other being and nothing else can. Therein is our joy and our distress at separation, the paradox of God's earthly schooling, which wishes above all other considerations to teach men and women to become eternally one.

Time cannot heal or fill her absence, for time has no voice, or smile, or heart. I do not anticipate it will—only that I will grow familiar with the loss as it becomes a natural part of my life, not as debilitating and raw as it is now, but in attendance all the same. What can I place in that empty center that her presence once filled? Hours? Months? Years? The only replacement for the absence of Laurie is Laurie. Nothing can truly make up the loss of those we love, and in some sense it would be unwise to attempt to do so. Endurance is what God asks of us, and endure we must, but need not be a distressing endurance. We hold on until reunion ends our wanting. It is not easy, but we feel the love while we wait, and love is always a good thing to fill a heart. God himself cannot replace the absence, nor do I believe He wishes to do so. Though He would soothe the wound, complete healing is not the desired outcome. Leaving it tender preserves the seal between us, draws us ever toward each other again. All this even at the terrible price of some of our bitterest tears. Death has taught me thus. Please do not misunderstand: happiness may be found within the bonds of new relationships, but those will be formed in open places of an expanding heart, without invading the sanctity of love already lodged there.

I do not fear death anymore, though I felt its dreaded footfalls each day I woke and looked at my wife sleeping beside me. My own passing will bring reunion, which reunion is now my most sincere prayer. I do not pray for death, nor wish it to come for me early, but for the assurance of eternal oneness with Laurie. Since death is the portal to the flowering of that oneness, when it comes I will not turn from it. I once viewed it from the perspective of the plan of salvation; now it is personal.

Upon the death of his wife, poet Robert Browning's whole view of dying changed, particularly as it awaited him at some future date. It was not something he feared; rather, he welcomed it, not in anticipation but in the culmination it would effect. He wrote the following words, which so wonderfully expressed how I now feel myself. They are from a poem titled "Prospice," which means "to look forward." Laurie and I had loved the ending to this poem before as we had read it together. It speaks depth of emotion to me now. I quoted it to Laurie during the last days of her life as a testimony to my own future. At that time she could not move or speak but could still listen. She was also able to still shed tears, which became at the end her only way of communicating. Her tears told me she understood.

> *I was ever a fighter, so-one fight more,*
> *The best and the last!*
> *I would hate that death bandaged my eyes, and forbore,*
> *And bade me creep past.*
> *No! let me taste the whole of it, fare like my peers*
> *The heroes of old,*
> *Bear the brunt, in a minute pay glad life's arrears*
> *Of pain, darkness and cold.*
> *For sudden, the worst turns the best to the brave,*
> *The black minutes at end,*
> *And the elements' rage, the fiend voices that rave,*
> *Shall dwindle, shall blend,*
> *Shall change, shall become first a peace out of pain,*
> *Then a light, then thy breast,*

O thou soul of my soul! I shall clasp thee again,
And with God be the rest.

Is it possible that death can be beautiful because so much love is born anew, refreshed in the heart like spring rain on green grass or the dew on waxed petals? If she's waiting, when I see her again, heaven will not be disappointing. It is not really "many mansions," celestial glory, or galactic splendor as some everlasting rewards I desire. They will all come after with her. She is the vital link. She is all that matters. Can anything else hold eternity together?

Editors' Take: This chapter was originally published by S. Michael Wilcox in his Deseret Book publication *Sunset: On the Passing of Those We Love.* The book is a wonderful treatise dealing with the loss of a loved one, and recommended to widows and widowers. Republished with permission of the author.

"Everybody in this life has their challenges and difficulties. That is part of our mortal test. The reason for some of these trials cannot be readily understood except on the basis of faith and hope because there is often a larger purpose which we do not always understand. Peace comes through hope." (James E. Faust)

Chapter Twenty-Four

The Big Elephant

BY SUSAN EASTON BLACK

Editors' Note: The loss of a spouse happens to a great many members of the Church, be they General Authorities, authors, celebrities, scholars, or any other good people. Death really is no respecter of persons.

It's just a wart," the family doctor said. "Nothing to worry about. There's no need for a biopsy." Two weeks later when another "wart" surfaced on the back of my husband's leg, he made an appointment with a dermatologist. The dermatologist biopsied the growth and within a few days reported signs of an aggressive sarcoma cancer. An appointment was made with a noted sarcoma cancer specialist in Salt Lake City. Seven surgeries followed, the last taking my husband's leg. The hopeful words, "His margins are clear" had become as repetitive as the cancer, radiation, and chemotherapy. The Huntsman Cancer Center was now our home away from home. Wheelchairs, blood transfusions, and handicap parking spaces had become as essential as life itself. Social outings and family gatherings, which had been a big part of our lives, were no more. Irritations that had been topics of discussion in past years were not even mentioned. Cancer was the "big elephant" in any conversation and present in every room. For five years, my husband suffered from the effects of cancer and the medical procedures to eradicate the cancer. And in so many ways, I suffered with him.

Being a caregiver leaves little room for selfish tendencies. None of my years of schooling or employment had prepared me for how to administer shots or operate oxygen equipment. Knowing when to call 911 or when to handle the emergency myself always was a question. The telephone numbers of a variety of healthcare personnel filled my address book, replacing the names of friends on "speed dial." Friends and even family members had to take a backseat to people who, a few years before, were not even acquaintances. Before long loved ones had stopped calling or coming to the house to visit. Some explained that they wanted to remember my husband as the robust man he had once been. Others had moved on to new friends. Yet there were those who stepped forward and became my support system, none more helpful than my Relief Society president, a former emergency room nurse.

I could have felt sorry for myself, but there wasn't much time for personal reflection. There were doctors' appointments to keep and health providers entering the home on a daily basis. To say that my world had turned upside down would be an understatement. Chores, which my husband

easily done around the house and yard, were now mine—
pumping gas into the car was the most awkward. There was
so much to do and so little time to complete any task before
the next emergency reared.

Neither of us gave up hope that the sarcoma cancer
would be eradicated until a physician pronounced after five
years of treatments, "The cancer has spread to his lungs and
brain. There is nothing more that can be done."

The funeral was lovely or at least that is what everyone said. The flowers were beautiful and the coffin, the
finest. The children spoke of their love for their father and
the bishop outlined the eternal plan of salvation, assuring
me, "The Lord needed your husband at this time." After
the funeral, when close family members and well-wishers
returned to their homes, I went to bed and tried to imagine
my future but came up short. For five years, my life had
been on hold. Now it lay before me with endless possibilities, but none looked joyful. Where was the meaning in life
without my husband?

The first week, there were thank-you notes to write and
offers from well-meaning friends to manage my finances.
The second week, I began to receive phone calls from
would-be suitors. At age twenty, such calls were flattering.
In my late sixties, even the suggestion of a romantic encounter scared me. I put an alarm system in the house and began
checking caller ID before answering the telephone. I hired
a "my girl Friday" to do simple things around the house,
mostly for companionship, and relied heavily upon my children for emotional support. Looking back on my situation,

I was somewhat of a burden to my loved ones. One son heartily agrees and remembers telling me, "Mom, get a life. We all want you to be happy."

I wasn't happy sitting on the back row of the chapel with the other widows in my ward. It was uncomfortable, yet I knew my place and tried to make the best of it. Fortunately, I had responsibilities that demanded my attention. In addition to my full-time work at BYU, I became a temple ordinance worker and a missionary volunteer for the LDS Social Services. Although I can honestly say that I crowded my life with good things, nothing made up for my incredible loss. I lamented to a close friend, "My husband doesn't even show up in my dreams." She replied, "It's just like him not to stay in touch." Although the elephant of cancer is now gone, eternity seems far away.

Editors' Take: Sadness and an incredible sense of loss come to those who lose a loved one, regardless of your testimony or understanding of the plan of salvation and the gospel.

"If we looked at mortality as the whole of existence, then pain, sorrow, failure, and short life would be calamity. But if we look upon life as an eternal thing stretching far into the pre-mortal past and on into the eternal post-death future, then all happenings may be put in proper perspective." (Spencer W. Kimball)

Chapter Twenty-Five

I Am a Priesthood Man

BY GEORGE DURRANT

Editors' Note: This is the story of how two people who were widowed met and married—the story of George Durrant and Susan Easton Black.

My son Matthew Durrant is the chief justice of the Utah State Supreme Court. It's a great thing to be a father. I dreamed of being a father. That was the only goal I could remember as a young man. Matthew was born while I was in the army. He cost us seven dollars. As he was growing up I often said to him, "You cost us seven dollars. But I want you to know something. You have been worth it."

Having a child is one thing and being a father is quite another. My greatest desire was to be a good father. We were able to have eight children. What a joy it was when Matt was born. I was able to go down to the hospital. In the army they wouldn't let me be in there when he was born, so I went down the hallway and looked in the glass and there he was.

I went in to see Marilyn, and I said to her, "I saw a baby and he looks just like me." She said, "Let's keep him anyway."

It was great being a father and a husband for all those years. Then I got to marry Susan. We've only been married four years now; that's because we waited until we got our student loans paid off.

After losing my beloved Marilyn I wondered, "What's next?" Every person's different, and one shouldn't really give advice to another. It's pretty dangerous, because no two people are alike. But for me, I wanted to marry again. I told my oldest daughter, "I'd like to date." She asked, "Who'd you like to date?" I said, "I'd like to date Susan Easton Black," who had just lost her husband. "The trouble is she's out of my league," I said. My daughter replied, "Father, no one is out of your league." That's what daughters are supposed to say.

I decided to drive over to Susan's house because she deserved the very best. On the way to see her, I decided to ask her to marry me. A timid young man from American Fork had become bold in old age. As I stood on her porch, knowing what I was about to do, I stood as straight as I could. I reminded myself that "I am a priesthood man." And with that I heard the pitter-patter of her feet as she came to the door.

She opened the door and looked surprised to see me. She said, "George, what brings you here?"

I said, "I've come to ask you to marry me."

She looked even more surprised and said, "Why don't you come inside and let's sit down and talk."

She has the reputation of being the smartest woman in the Church. I think you can see now another reason. After a year of using my most persuasive personality, she began to take me seriously. I took her to up to Kolob Canyon and on a rather high pinnacle, I said, "Either take the ring or I'm going to jump." Lucky for me, she had attended many Relief Society lessons on compassionate service.

I had the privilege of marrying Susan Easton Black. It's been four years of pure joy. What a delightful human being—what a kind woman. And I, frankly, I don't believe there has ever been a woman so in love with a man as she is with me. It's hard to understand, but I come back to my basic premise: I really try to be a priesthood man. I try to be kind and considerate. I can't always pull it off, but I want to. It's hard to bring everything good to the table.

I love you all. I know this Church is true. Some say they're leaving the Church because they're finding so many questions. I say, "I'm staying because I find so many answers."

What a joyous thing life is. I'm a sealer in the temple. If a marriage is kind of on the rocks and you could go see a marriage counselor or participate in sealings at a temple, which would do you the most good? I say, "Come to the temple, learn what marriage is all about." I know you are not all married, or all married happily. I'm not talking about being married, I'm talking about the ideal. It all comes through spirituality, not through materialism or anything else. Reach for that which is of greatest worth.

Editors' Take: Be positive and hopeful, and why not? The Lord loves you and wants the best for you.

"Our trials can either end up hardening our heart or humbling us. How true the saying that suffering in life is inevitable, but misery is of our own making. In other words, because of the plan that we all agreed upon in the premortal life, we are going to suffer, whether we want to or not. However, if you can find how to suffer that tribulation in the Redeemer's name, you will bear it well and perhaps even do it with an understanding, happy heart." (Gene R. Cook)

Chapter Twenty-Six

Single? Well, I Guess I Am, and I Guess So Is the Prophet

BY ANN NONYMOUS

Editors' Note: We can still feel married and still feel motivated to have good goals. (This article was written when President Monson was the President of the Church of Jesus Christ of Latter-day Saints and was widowed.)

The problem is I don't entirely think of myself as single. I think I am as married today as I was over six years ago before my husband died. But our "separation" is going on much too long. Enough already! It isn't easy to remember holding hands in church and to know that won't happen again in this life. It isn't easy to hear of couples I admire going on the trips we had planned and worked toward, yet will not be taking. It has been difficult to try to do the "male-oriented" jobs involved in keeping up a house and yard and car. It isn't easy to remember our Friday night dates and know that he is not concerned whether or not we should go see the latest feel-good Mormon movie, because he has more important things to do than see a mere movie about faith.

Seven years ago, my husband, who had retired from his CPA practice, undertook the project of finishing the basement in a home we had purchased. I was still working and planned to retire in one more year. He took a year to complete the finish work on three rooms up to his usual level of perfection, including the shop he had dreamed of having where he could do his carving and other projects. At the end of a year we moved into our new home. One month later he was diagnosed with colon cancer. The day after he was diagnosed, I quit my job to be with him. He was gone in two weeks.

So in about a six-week period, I lost my husband, my job, my home of twenty-five years, my ward, and my friends at church, at work, and in the neighborhood. No, I had not really lost some of these things, but they were beyond my grasp.

So here I am six years later, with no drug convictions, no DUIs, no psych ward commitments, no subsequent disastrous marriages based on desperate loneliness. And you are asking, what is my coping mechanism? I hope I can sift through my feelings and thoughts to come up with an answer.

I did not go through the eight phases of grieving (or however many there are). I did feel shock, extreme shock, for a long time. I didn't sleep well. In fact, I am still fearful or "shocky" at times.

I didn't start out with a plan. I just got through the days doing the many things that need to be done as a new widow. The financial dealings were quite foreign to me since my husband was a CPA and, of course, handled our finances. I was blessed with a son-in-law who was well educated in business and was willing to help me.

We had not yet furnished our new home, so the living room and the family room were empty rooms for many, many months until I could make the necessary decisions and have the furniture ordered. When our dear bishop visited me once and looked around at the empty space, he asked if I needed financial help. I didn't. But how kind of him to ask.

My great blessings came in the form of family and friends. My daughters and son and their spouses were there for me during my husband's two weeks in the hospital, the funeral, and after. My sister has been a tremendous help to me when I have something to do requiring more strength than I have. Together, we can get it done. She has also been my social life as we take trips, go to the theater, concerts, temple, and movies. We take care of our ninety-year-old mother, who now requires full-time care.

I have worked at the temple for the last six years. For the last three years I have tended my grandson two days a week while his mother teaches at Brigham Young University. One of my daughters has taught me how to do genealogy and we spend an inordinate amount of time on perfecting our records and getting the temple work done. And we love it!

I have been invited to join two different family home evening groups, one for single ladies and one a neighborhood couples group. In fact, I was invited to attend a Family Home Evening the Monday night after my husband was buried on Saturday. When I showed up, the hostess said, "We didn't expect you." These friends are very dear to me as are all the friends I have met during my six years of being "alone."

I have taken classes at UVU for the past nine years. I used to take classes for real, now I just audit. It costs only a tiny registration fee when you are sixty-two or older. I take classes that I am interested in with no regard to what is required for a degree. I don't care if they are upper or lower division. I only take one or two classes, but do all the homework. It is such a pleasure.

So, what have I learned from this experience? Maybe three things. First, how important it is to appreciate your mate. If I ever see or hear of a couple who are not in harmony with each other, I want to take them aside and tell them to wake up and stop to realize how precious their loved one is. I did appreciate my husband, but not enough. It's never enough.

Second, stay busy. I try to fill every day to capacity. I like to be tired enough at night so that I can barely close the book and turn off the light.

Third, I now realize how truly important the gospel is. I always believed it, but now it really matters that there is a Christ who has made the great sacrifice so that we can be resurrected and be together again. It really matters that we can have eternal life. It really matters that the gospel and its commandments are a great plan for our happiness. I am so thankful that I know this and that I know I can be a participant in all of Christ's blessings to us, if I work toward that goal.

A few years ago, I typed up my little goal sheet, my motto, my creed, my mission statement, or whatever we call these trite little sayings that succinctly define our goals for ourselves. It isn't holy or thought provoking or insightful; it is just a simple statement of how I am trying to live my life.

Today I should

1. Give some service to someone.
2. Learn something.
3. Take care of myself.
4. Appreciate my blessings.
5. Be happy.

Editors' Take: "Appreciate your mate. . . . I did appreciate my husband, but not enough. It's never enough."

"As you overcome adversity in your life, you will become stronger. Then you will be better able to help others—those who are working, in their turn, to find a safe harbor from the storms that rage about them." (Joseph B. Wirthlin)

Chapter Twenty-Seven

Forever Wilt Thou Love

BY S. MICHAEL WILCOX

Editors' Note: Dealing with grief is part of the human process, part of the "Become like God process," and part of life.

The challenge of writing about life-changing encoun-
ters is knowing when to cease. I fear to write or refine
much more lest the emotion become contrived or sincerity
compromised. I so earnestly desire honesty. Everything still
floats so near the surface of my heart, yet the time may soon
come when the learning sinks into the depths of memory and
drawing it upwards again with clarity becomes too difficult
a labor. The journey we began that April night can only end
with behind-the-veil redresses. It goes on, as life must go
on and move forward with "brightness of hope." Grief has
become my companion, though not entirely unwelcome, for
he carves the hollow that one day love and Laurie will fill

with joy. If the wound be deep, the balm that heals it will be all the sweeter. Then will come that yearning, enduring gratitude to our God whose concern for these human hearts of ours found a way.

I know there will be difficult days ahead. For the time being, I am running, through the busyness of my life and constant occupation of my time, to stay one reach ahead of grief's most fatal footfalls. I must go through her things soon, and decisions will be made. The dress she wore on those magic nights I will keep with its whisper of perfume. Her hairbrush with a few long strands still caught within its bristles, the pencils she drew with, the music she sang in the Holy Land, pieces of oft-worn jewelry, the golden navigator's compass she gave me one Christmas, and the books with her underlinings or straying pen marks will stay with me. And, of course, there are the pictures and the notes and cards in which I can still hear her voice. All these, and others I shall discover in the awaiting days, will bring the poignant, sweet aching of memory. All who grieve will keep those things that draw the beloved's presence nearer. They are healing. They increase as well as maintain the bond. They will be different for each of us, and the simplest object may bring the strongest ties.

I struggled hard with the decision, but ended up keeping her wedding ring. There was a certain stab of nostalgia in removing it. I hope I made the right choice. The inscription we placed in hers is coupled with the one in mine, and I could not see it go into the ground. It is a line from Keats that I had the good fortune to be studying when I proposed:

"Forever wilt thou love, and she be fair." I could not have imagined when I had the first four words of that verse engraved in my ring and the last four in hers how appropriate they would remain and the smile they would bring in our current parting. She is fairer now than she ever was in life. And my love will certainly be forever. She lost her contact lens the night I gave the ring to her, and we spent fifteen minutes looking for it before she could see her diamond and read the engravings. How often did we laugh over that memory!

I will face the first year's difficult anniversaries—which may not become less tender or sore with the accumulation of successive years, yet the joyful ones must remain joyful and not sink into loneliness. Our wedding day was the happiness moment of my life and so it will remain. I will continue to ask myself, "Where are you now, Laurie? What are you doing today? How do you feel? What are you thinking? What memories bless you or haunt you? The last I pray you forget. Can you hear me when I talk to you? I tell you I love you every day and all that you mean to me. Is your love growing for me as mine is for you?" I will continue to talk to her with the same casual reverence of whispered prayer, sometimes shifting from my Father in Heaven to Laurie and back again in mid conversation. I don't supposed the Lord minds such intimate sharing or lovely company. If she can't receive my words, I ask God, who can, to tell her all I feel?

"Tell her, Lord, that she was the loveliest thing my eyes ever rested upon, that the greatest happinesses of my life were

centered in her. She was my best friend, and I will always love her."

Even the smallest actions or memories may surprise us with their pull. I shall not forget the first time I returned to the house and the truth struck me like a blow that she was not there. I will walk those places we dreamed of visiting together and listen for a footstep or change in the breeze to let me know she is with me if only fleetingly, longing to hear again the excitement in her voice: "Who would have thought that a small-town Alberta girl would be standing here!"

I will know her loss in the faces of my children and grandchildren and in the voices of her friends. The unexpected and unaccounted for will surely come, leaving me, at least initially, with no defenses. Rising sorrow will break once again into sobbing or quiet tears. How it stung to circle the "w" for widower on an entry visa less than two weeks after her death, or to receive four days after the funeral a well-intentioned invitation in the mail to attend a singles' activity for those widowed, or to hear a good friend say—I'm sure meaning it consolingly—"Of course, you'll remarry." Does the ring I wear on my finger with its four cherished words tell me I am still married? And I've never said good-bye.

Hearing: "Only one?" or "Just you?" when checking in for a flight or being seated at a restaurant will never feel normal. It's as if others are as surprised as I am that Laurie is not standing next to me. I no longer carry her passport, or help her search for her sunglasses, or place her feet on the rests of the wheelchair, or make her eggs and orange juice for breakfast—but I wake to her picture on the nightstand by my bed, the first thing I greet each morning.

There are bright spots, too. Her hand remained quite warm in mine right up to the last gentle breaths. There was no creeping chill. The beautiful music and thoughts shared at her funeral and the continual pouring out of love by so many concerned friends stay soft and comforting. I discovered anew the last note she wrote me with its broken thoughts and apologetic tone—"I'm sorry to go by Kirsten's today but I'm got to play for by myself . . ."—because she drove the car when she knew her medical condition forbade it. But she ended the note with, "I love you, and I'll be back. All my love, Laurie." I thank God that the cancer could not confuse *that* message. Comfort on a scrap of paper!

There was the dreaded next-day visit to the cemetery, yet I found her grave covered with hundreds of flowers, unwilted, frozen fresh in their spring colors with the white frost of the mountains reflecting the winter sun. The gift of friends! Here was a touch of May on a January morning. Warm memories and even laughter are surfacing in the drawers and closets that contained what she gathered and saved over the years. She rarely threw anything away and was often afraid I would. There are little notes with exclamation points following them stating emphatically, "DON'T THROW AWAY!"

I have felt her passing draw my children closer into my heart, and friends have become dearer to me. It has also been a long time since prayer has meant so much or the temple been such a necessity. We must learn to meet the good and the bad, the tender and the remorse-filled moments day by day as they come. We do not face them all at once. Both are expressions of our love.

Editors' Note: This chapter was originally published by S. Michael Wilcox in his Deseret Book publication *Sunset: On the Passing of Those We Love*. Republished with permission.

"Hold on thy way . . . Thy days are known, and thy years shall not be numbered less; therefore fear not what man can do, for God shall be with you forever and ever." (D&C 122:9)

Chapter Twenty-Eight

The Privilege

BY SCOT ALLEN

Editors' Note: A talk given at the Draper Eastridge Stake Conference on February 12, 2006.

Why do I get the privilege of speaking today? It really is a privilege, and I will get back to that question in a few minutes. Let me start by telling a story about my beautiful wife, Kim.

On July 15, 2003, we learned that she had two tennis ball–sized tumors in her liver. Over the next two years, Kim had four major surgeries, including the complete removal of her right lung because there was a tumor in that lung. During these two years, Kim also went through six months of intense chemotherapy. She also had twenty-eight radiation treatments to her abdomen. The cancer later spread to her brain in the form of seven brain tumors. Kim withstood ten more radiation treatments to her head for these tumors.

On July 31, 2005, Kim passed away peacefully at home with her loved ones standing around her.

Today happens to be Kim's birthday. Standing here in front of you today is a great way to honor Kim by speaking about a subject that she and I both love dearly: the gospel of Jesus Christ. More specifically, I will be speaking about how we can endure through our trials. This is why I consider it a great privilege to be here.

Through the course of Kim's illness, she suffered greatly. At times, I wondered if we were doing the right things in her treatments. I now feel that we did. I know that she lived longer than she would have. By living longer, she became, as Elder Scott said, "an instrument through which the Lord can bless another" (Elder Richard G. Scott, May 1994 general conference, "To Be Healed"). Kim blessed many. Though she suffered greatly, not once did she complain or say, "Why is this happening to me?" She was a pillar of faith. Kim had very strong faith. She knew that everything would be okay. She put her trust in the Lord and knew that He was in control.

Since Kim died, I have had several people ask me how I have been able to remain faithful in church attendance and my callings with the loss of my wife. All I can say is that the Church was true before she died, and it is just as true now. My entire life, my goal was to be able to live with our Heavenly Father and Jesus Christ again. Now that goal has increased. I want to do whatever I have to do in order to be with Kim again.

How do we gain faith necessary to endure our trials? For those of us fortunate enough to have the gospel at an early age, it started then. I have two great parents, as does Kim. They are all here today watching my three little girls while I speak. My parents led by example in showing the importance of living the gospel. I remember it was never a question if we would attend our church meetings or not. Since it is a commandment that we attend, we just did. I remember that it was never a question of whether or not we pay tithing. Since it is a commandment, we just did. There are many other examples I could list. Each of us, as parents, has the responsibility to teach our children these things. As we grow and learn, our faith will grow. We need to build our faith to the point that if we have trials, which we all will, we can draw on that faith to help us through. Just doing a few good things to build our faith is not enough. President Eyring said that "great faith has a short shelf life" (Elder Henry B. Eyring, October 2005 general conference, "Spiritual Preparedness: Start Early and Be Steady"). The faith you have will dwindle if you do not constantly work on keeping it built up.

We have many resources that we can use to build our faith up and keep it strong. I will now list some of these:

1. Scriptures. They are very important. One verse that I read last night in my scripture study goes along well with this talk. In Alma 36:3, Alma is speaking to his son, Helaman. He says, "I beseech of thee that thou wilt hear my words and learn of me; for I do know that whosoever shall put

their trust in God shall be supported in their trials, and their troubles, and their afflictions, and shall be lifted up at the last day." This is exactly what Kim did, and what we each should do. If we will study, not just read, the scriptures regularly, we will receive answers to our everyday problems. This will increase our faith.

2. Prophets and Apostles. We receive modern-day revelation through them. We must listen to their words always. Where do we hear from them? The *Ensign* magazine. Their words are often referred to as modern scripture. General conference talks. We should listen to every session. Proclamations, such as "The Proclamation to the Family."

3. Patriarchal Blessings. With mine, after I got married I almost felt that everything in the blessing has been fulfilled. As I read it more and more I realize that the blessing is continually being fulfilled. Kim and I read through hers frequently during her illness, and we were comforted many times. Now as I read her blessing, since she died, I can see that she is exactly where she is supposed to be now, and she is very busy on the other side. The patriarchal blessing is a road map to what we can do and become if we will remain faithful. Reading it frequently and thoughtfully will build our faith.

4. Other priesthood blessings. Through the course of Kim's illness she was given many blessings, from me and many other worthy priesthood holders. I saw many miracles performed through the power of the priesthood. One miracle that seems simple happened frequently. There were many times in the middle of the night when I would wake up

and could hear Kim sobbing, but trying to be silent so she would not wake me up. She was in tremendous pain. I would give her a blessing, and within a few minutes she was fine and could sleep through the night. I want to relate two experiences that deal with how fathers' blessings have built faith in my girls. Each year before school starts I give my daughters their own blessing. When my now six-year-old, Kelsey, was starting preschool I gave her a blessing. I didn't realize until months later how it affected her. She told me that she had been very scared to start preschool, but after the blessing she was no longer scared. She ended up enjoying her preschool experience. A few months ago my three-year-old, Kaitlyn, was sick and not able to sleep. She asked me for a blessing as I had done many times before for her mommy. She slept through the night and let everyone know the next morning that it was because of the blessing. We need to ask for these blessings when we feel we need them. They will build our faith.

5. Our local church leaders. I have learned that President Becerra and Bishop Pulsipher are truly inspired. They are great men with special callings. I love them very much.

There are many other resources we have for building our faith. These are just a few of the ones that have become very personal to me.

If we will do all we can to follow our Heavenly Father's plan, we will build up the faith necessary to endure our trials. But as with everything else in the plan, we still have a choice as to whether we will endure or not. I challenge everyone here to make the right choice as we go through our trials. Instead of blaming anyone, including our Heavenly Father, for putting us through the trial, whether it be the death of a loved one, or financial difficulties, or anything else, choose to put your trust in the Lord, and He *will* support you through your trials.

In conclusion, I want to thank President Becerra for giving me this opportunity to stand and speak today. To be perfectly honest, speaking absolutely terrifies me, but it also builds my faith and makes me a better person. I know he was inspired to call me to do this.

I want to bear my testimony. I know that this great work we are engaged in, even the gospel of Jesus Christ, is true. The Book of Mormon is true. The words found within were written for us in these latter days. We need to read these words, and study them. I know that Joseph Smith was and is a true prophet and that through him the gospel was restored in its fullness. I know that we have a true prophet today, President Gordon B. Hinckley, and that he does receive revelation to guide us now. I want to tell my girls, Ashley, Kelsey, and Kaitlyn, how much I love them. I am amazed and strengthened by their faith. They frequently mention that they are very excited to see their mommy again after they grow old and die. They don't question whether they will see her or not; they know that they will. I am grateful for the gospel and the plan of happiness contained within. It is a plan that will end in happiness if we will but endure to the end. I know our Savior, Jesus Christ, took upon Himself our sins and our suffering. Our lives will be much easier if we will but look to Him and put our lives in His hands. I love the gospel. I am looking forward to the day that I will be with my Kim again, and we will progress through the eternities as a family unit. I say these things in the name of Jesus Christ, amen.

Editors' Take: "Choose to put your trust in the Lord, and He *will* support you through your trials."

"It isn't as bad as you sometimes think it is.
It all works out. Don't worry.
I say that to myself every morning.
It will all work out.
Put your trust in God,
and move forward with faith
and confidence in the future.
The Lord will not forsake us.
He will not forsake us.
If we will put our trust in Him,
if we will pray to Him,
if we will live worthy of His blessings,
He will hear our prayers."
(Gordon B. Hinckley, from the funeral program for Marjorie Pay Hinckley, April 10, 2004)

Chapter Twenty-Nine

The Race

BY CARMEN CRANE

Editors' Note: A talk given at the Draper Eastridge Stake Conference 2007.

I remember attending this same conference last year. My husband and three boys and I were sitting in the gym about halfway back. I remember the brother that gave a talk about losing his wife. I remember thinking how sad that must have been and amazed at how he dealt with this trial. Little did I know that in just six short days I would be faced with the same challenge.

My husband, Stan, died very unexpectedly at the age of thirty-three of a fatal heart condition we didn't know he had. We had just come home from a date and had settled into bed and were watching TV when I fell asleep and the next thing I knew, he called my name. I woke up to see what he wanted and he wasn't breathing. I called 911 and they rushed him to the hospital. At 1:17 AM on Feb. 18, 2006, they pronounced him dead. At that moment, my life as I knew it was over. I had just become a thirty-one-year-old widow with three boys to raise on my own.

I am going to use an analogy to describe to you what happened after that. I enjoy running. It was while I was running that I thought of this analogy.

Life is like a marathon. Stan and I and the boys were running along in the race of life. We were feeling great, running at a good pace and life was good. All of a sudden, Stan crossed the finish line. My first thought was that he isn't really gone; he has just gone to the porta-potty. But when reality set in, I decided to sit on the side of the road and cry. I was angry! This was not how life was supposed to turn out for me! I questioned the Lord's wisdom in taking Stan instead of me; after all, he could do this much better than I could. I was mad at families that had dads. I wanted to stick my foot out and trip happy families going past that had dads so they could feel as bad as I was feeling. All I could think about was me and how bad I was feeling.

I finally realized that I had two choices: Either I could stay here on the side of the road and feel sorry for myself the rest of my life or I could have faith and stand up and start taking small steps.

Well, when you prepare for a race you have to train for it. There are no Olympians who got a gold medal the first time they raced. They trained for many years to become so good. They didn't just practice once every other week or month. They trained daily. The same is true for us in our race of life. We must train daily. We must decide what is most important. Do we want to have a good race or not? I knew that in order for me to stand and face the steep hill that was ahead of me, I was going to have to step up my training a notch. I was going to have to study my scriptures, not just read them, but study them, every day. I was going to need to attend the temple as often as possible. I was going to have family prayer and family scripture study every day. My goal was to make sure my boys didn't walk out that door for school without first reading their scriptures and having family prayer. I needed now, more than ever, to be worthy of personal revelation and promptings from the Holy Ghost. I wanted to be spiritually well-trained. I wanted to be able to hear the Coach. I haven't been perfect, but I have seen a difference in the way I have felt. I challenge each of you to examine where your training is at. Are you training your very best?

I knew I wasn't going to start off by sprinting or even running, let alone jogging. It was amazing what happened when I made the choice to get up. All of a sudden the view became much different. There were so many people there to help; in fact, they had been there all along but because I had been so focused on me and my sorrow, I didn't even notice them. Friends, family, and neighbors were all there to cheer me on. Some were running next to me, others handing me a water bottle when I needed one, others wiping my brow, some patting me on the back, others handing out energy gels. Some would even carry the boys for a while so I could run by myself.

As I look back on this past year, the amazing thing to see is how much I was carried by the Savior. He didn't just carry me and the boys a few steps; He carried me for many miles. In Matthew 11:28–30 it says: "Come unto me all ye that labor and are heavy laden and I will give you rest. Take my yoke upon you. For my yoke is easy and my burden is light." That scripture has a whole new meaning for me now. He has taught me so much this year; things I couldn't have learned any other way. I am a different person than I was a year ago sitting in the gym about halfway back.

I find comfort in knowing that I don't have to run this race alone. In Alma 26, Ammon talks of rejoicing in the Lord. The Lord knows how we feel because He's already run this race. He can comfort us and help us to the end. I feel like Ammon when I think to myself how many people are running this race alone without any cheerleaders and with no help along the way. I could never do this on my own and therefore I, like Ammon, rejoice! He sad, "My heart is brim with joy. . . . For in his strength I can do all things . . . we will praise his name forever" (Alma 26:11–12).

I have realized how much Heavenly Father knows me, how much He loves me and is aware of me. He cares about all of my smallest, tiniest concerns. He is in the details. He has blessed me with so many "tender mercies" this year.

I am comforted in knowing that Stan is at the finish line waiting for me to finish my race. He is cheering me and the boys on. Our challenge is to endure to the end no matter how many hills, side aches, or blisters we encounter. I challenge each of you that when you are faced with hills or even mountains in your race of life that you will have faith to keep going. That you will choose to cling to the Savior and as you do, you will have "reason to rejoice."

The Atonement of Jesus Christ is not just for sinners; it is for all of us to find peace and solace during this chaotic race we call mortality.

I want you to know that I have a testimony. I am so grateful for this gospel, I have a testimony of the Book of Mormon, and I know that Joseph Smith translated it and that he was a true prophet. I know that President Hinckley is the prophet today. I am so thankful now more than ever for my temple marriage and that I know I am sealed to Stan. I am so grateful for the Savior and for His atoning sacrifice for me. He is the one who made it possible for me to one day be reunited with Stan.

Editors' Take: There are many wanting to help us through our trials if we let them, and if we open our eyes to what they are trying to do for us and to what the Lord has done for us.

"And now, I hope it is clearer why part of that hope in Christ is hope in the future, a future that includes resurrection and salvation and exaltation. He is my hope on rainy Monday mornings, my hope on dark nights, and my hope in the face of death and despair." (Chieko N. Okazaki)

Chapter Thirty

A Weeping Joy

BY S. MICHAEL WILCOX

Editors' Note: There is much joy to be found in the release of a loved one from the pains of this life.

All of the challenges became more bearable two nights after her death when the midnight thoughts were halted and made to retreat, though not banished from the field. On that night I first experienced the balm of a weeping joy. It really wasn't so profound an experience—quite simple, actually. It was just the thought growing into an assurance and finally lodging in my being that life's adversities were completed for Laurie. She had reached the ending place. By that I did not mean just the eight months of cancer, but all the pain she had fought during the last ten years of her life; it meant what we refer to as the testing or proving of mortality. She was free of it all. As Jesus on the cross said of the pains and purposes of His life, "It is finished" (John 19:30), so too was it finished for my Laurie. She had endured enough pain in mortality to enjoy more deeply the happiness and rest of eternity. I pray she will experience as much joy as her merry heart can feel.

Gratitude swept over me, into me, all around me, and I wept for the first time with joy, joy at her release. I felt myself smiling again. It was over, all of it was over! How wonderful for her! For the time I was not conscious of my own hurting. I don't recall ever feeling such joy in another's happiness. My pain was swallowed up in the gladness for her. She mattered most of all; for the moment I was inconsequential. It was that "gush of compassion," that swelling of selfless love contained in a beloved Hindu parable which I had frequently taught. It was a taste of the Buddha's "Nirvana," the state where pain is ended in the total outward vision of the soul that feels only for others, not for self. It was Christianity's definition of charity, the love that "seeketh not her own" (1 Corinthians 13:5). It was insight into the pure love of Christ, and how soothing to an aching soul it was. I wept as hard that night as I had ever wept in grief. How happy I was for her! I thanked God for ending her trials and accepting her into His own care. It was not as hard knowing she was passing into His guardianship. I could let her go.

The feelings lasted throughout the night, and for the first time since that awful April day, the midnight stirrings had to hide from the light of compassionate, selfless joy. I knew at that same moment that she would also want me to be cheerful and to delight in the relationships and experiences that were left to me in life. I cannot always bring back the weeping joy, but the memory of how I felt that night, the emotion of it all, as well as the reasoning, can still hold at bay the night thoughts. I will weep for the loss of her touch, her voice, her presence, but at least now there is a smile behind the tears, one that remains with me, as constant a companion and comforter as the Holy Spirit. Maybe it is the Holy Spirit.

Editors' Note: This chapter was originally published by S. Michael Wilcox in his Deseret Book publication *Sunset: On the Passing of Those We Love*. Republished with permission.

"Adversity has the effect of eliciting talents, which in prosperous circumstances would have lain dormant." (Horace)

Chapter Thirty-One

Making Sense of Suffering (excerpts)

BY WAYNE E. BRICKEY

Editors' Note: These thoughts are powerful insights that may help in coping with the loss of a loved one.

T he God of perfect love is a God of perfect wisdom, and he is nearby. But his plan permits suffering in his universe. Without apology, he keeps sending his spirit children into the thick of things. In his long view, suffering makes sense. It can never make much sense to us, however, until we see things his way." (p. 1)

"God grants mortal suffering because it can do wonders for us." (p. 2)

"Mortal suffering makes lasting improvements in the eternal self. It turns up the volume on God's voice to us, and it turns up the volume on our pleading to him." (p. 2)

"What would be the use of an easy and forgettable mortal life?" (p. 5)

"Suffering places us behind a door and hides us somewhat from the view of others. The privacy allows adjustments, renewal, and transformation." (p. 10)

"He who asks for our little 'all' will greet us after our return to him and will give us his infinite 'all.'" (p. 11)

"The word can transform us but only when we are ready. Tribulation often precedes the voice of God, in Church history and in private life. The foundation is not laid in easy steps." (p. 14)

"Trials are explorations of strength. But because they stretch us, trials do not just check for strength, they add strength. Trials also deepen our search for depth. Trials do this for the innocent as well as for the guilty." (p. 24)

"When others help us heal, they too may suffer in some way. Suffering is the modest price of real friendship. Parents, leaders, and teachers who quietly pay this price day and night for their children and their charges are true friends." (p. 25)

"When we suffer, let us see the passing present as it is—destined to become a small part of the combined yesterdays." (p. 40)

"Whatever the outward task, the inner taming is our real work." (p. 45)

"The patience of faith is called long-suffering. . . . Patience does not mind waiting. It bends meekly before the necessary and stands firm before the unnecessary, never cowering or pouting. It inherits the earth. Nothing quite compares to the rest and freedom of a life lived in patient faith." (p. 51)

"We respond to good cheer in this world because of our long history with light in the life before. Thus, children naturally believe that things will be okay. But anxiety, the denial of light, erodes our original cheery nature. Pain invites us to doubt the 'okay' approach to things. If we accept that invitation, a chain of anxieties will follow. . . . One anxiety in that chain is the fear of further pain: 'How long will this last?' And an even more terrifying and misleading link is, 'This wasn't supposed to happen.' Our fond plans seem holy to us as if they were the very plans of God. Timid doubt thinks perhaps God himself has lost control. And yet another anxiety may erupt: 'No one cares.' Self-centered, self-deceiving, and self-defeating, anxiety robs us of good cheer and chains us to a dungeon floor. . . ." (pp. 54–55)

"The truth is, our troubles are not so mighty when viewed from eternity. We preceded the world and will long outlive it." (p. 55)

Editors' Take: Trials are the means by which we grow to become more like our Savior. The excerpts shared in this chapter are from the book, *Making Sense of Suffering,* published in 2001 by Deseret Book Company. Used with permission.

"As we pursue our journeys, let us ever bear in mind that in train travel and in life, there are stations, there are departures, calls, schedules, and opportunities for being side-tracked and diverted. Wise is the individual who follows in his, the Savior's, paths. Safety and joy belong to those who will come and follow him. I bear witness to you today that God is eternal. We are eternal, and God never intended for us to travel alone." (Marvin J. Ashton)

Section Five

Final Thoughts

"No matter how serious the trial, how deep the distress, how great the affliction, [God] will never desert us. He never has, and He never will. He cannot do it. It is not His character. He is an unchangeable being; the same yesterday, the same today, and He will be the same throughout the eternal ages to come. We have found that God. We have made Him our friend, by obeying His Gospel; and He will stand by us. We may pass through the fiery furnace; we may pass through deep waters; but we shall not be consumed nor overwhelmed. We shall emerge from all these trials and difficulties the better and purer for them, if we only trust in our God and keep His commandments." (George Q. Cannon)

Chapter Thirty-Two

Hope You Find What You Are Looking For

BY MICHAEL AGRELIUS

Editors' Note: Conclusions regarding findings we make when we "find" ourselves alone.

As you have gathered from the stories here, feeling lonely and finding yourself alone are two very different things. You can feel lonely almost anywhere or in any situation, with friends, in a marriage, or in a crowded church meeting.

The phrase "finding myself alone" is powerful, not depressing, for a number of reasons. First, it is an "action" phrase. *Finding* can indicate the object of a search. It also implies "discovery." There are tremendous opportunities that being alone affords us.

Firstly, the words "finding myself alone" appear to be a key to unlocking the answers to questions that we have when we are confused or discouraged. "Finding myself" is a worthy and virtuous activity to engage in when one is alone. There is something wonderfully positive, hopeful, and comforting in those words. The phrase suggests an ongoing journey or event, that "finding" oneself is a process.

Secondly, "finding myself alone" can be a discovery and a preparation for enlightenment and revelation. The phrase is scripturally based (JS—H 1:15) and, like most scripture, is very poetic and can be appreciated on many different levels. Joseph Smith and other prophets often sought time to ponder the things of God on their own, prior to receiving revelations. A period of preparation when one is alone seems a necessity, at least that appears to be the case for Moses, the Savior, and Joseph Smith prior to the commencement of their respective ministries.

Lastly but most importantly, maybe it is in *finding God first* that opens the door to finding ourselves. Developing a relationship with God is an individual journey. It is often a venture that is better accomplished on your own and without others to distract you.

To have the knowledge that *He is there beside us in all we do*, that He is our Father and He knows each of our names, our individual hopes, our disappointments, our dreams, our potential, is worth all the tests, tears, and trials we must go through. Those answers seem to come to people more frequently when they are alone. In those quiet and contemplative moments of solitude we often realize that we really aren't alone; we never were alone. If we look, we will see. If we seek, we will find. If we are still, we will know. *"Be still, and know that I am God."* (Psalms 46:10)

And it is after we are on sure ground with the Lord that we can invite others to join us on the path.

It would be naive and mistaken to suggest that being alone is the object or design of our existence. We are all aware that after He created Adam, the Almighty declared, "It is not good that the man should be alone" (Genesis 2:18). Adam and his wife Eve were married prior to death being introduced into the world (see Genesis 2:24–25). Their union was to be forever. The concept of "death do they part" was not in their minds or in the mind of Him who had married them. Not being alone in the eternities transcends being "just married." Most people know in their hearts that there is more to it, more to hope for than to be "just married."

We cannot be saved without our dead (see Malachi 4:5–6 and D&C 128) or exalted by ourselves (see D&C 132). However, there does seem to be evidence to suggest that when we, on occasion, find ourselves alone we can learn fundamental truths about our own nature and mission, receive powerful and personal revelations, and grow in our relationship with God. Through these opportunities for tremendous growth, we prepare ourselves for the rich blessings that Heavenly Father has in store for us.

When Spirits Meet in Flesh

From unknown corridors in unseen worlds—
    Spirits calculated, dreamed, and planned.
Friends in eternities sought opportunities—
    To pinpoint a moment, a place, a time—
    In a finite future where they could meet—
    And discover each other and the knowledge they had.

When spirits meet in an airport, or a bus,
    On a crowded street in the heart of the city—
    There's recognition for a moment—
    When intangibles converge and senses are halted—
    To allow the soul to zero in on this gift of FEELING.
If ignored it retreats, as if the plan was never made—
    And opportunities are lost—
    As if eternities didn't matter—
    And dreams were just dreams—
    As if the present really is all there is.
But . . .
    When spirits meet in the flesh, on course—
    There's a spark of familiarity, and an instant of excitement–

That can expand into a fire of life so intense—
    That mortality is mundane and pedestrian at best.

There's a chemistry beyond the temporal—
    It reaches back to a history before this world—
    It touches deep in molecules you didn't know were there.

All of a sudden, the world, your life, your future—
    It all makes sense.

Knowledge fills the soul, compassion fills your being.

There is a rebirth and awakening.

And you are at one.

—m. agrelius

"And it came to pass that we lived after the manner of happiness." (2 Nephi 5:27)

Share Your Story

Do you have a story to share of being alone? If so, share your story with us for consideration in Volume 2 of *Finding Myself Alone* at taylor.halverson@gmail.com.

About the Authors

Mike Agrelius

Mike Agrelius is a poet, game designer, author of the children's picture book, *Hear What's Here*, and former travel executive. He got married for the first time at age 31, divorced at age 49, and remarried at age 58. He says the best advice he received was on his wedding day, "Be nice to each other."

Taylor Halverson

Taylor Halverson is an aspiring master learner who loves people, laughter, telling stories, and learning. Many friends call him a walking encyclopedia, but he may be best known for having fallen down the Outhouse. Lucky for him it was a ski run at a Colorado ski resort. Taylor works full time at BYU as a teaching and learning expert and lives in Springville, Utah, with his wife and two kids. Learn more at taylorhalverson.com.

Would you like a free humorous ebook from Taylor? Go here to request *Memoirs of The Ward Rumor Control Coordinator*: shorturl.at/koqO5

Printed in Poland
by Amazon Fulfillment
Poland Sp. z o.o., Wrocław